The **12** Clichés *of* Selling
[*and* why they work]

by **BARRY FARBER**

WORKMAN PUBLISHING • NEW YORK

Library of Congress Cataloging-in-Publication Data

Farber, Barry.

   The 12 clichés of selling : and why they work / Barry Farber.
     p. cm.

   ISBN 0-7611-1697-4 (alk. paper)
   1.Selling. I. Title: The Twelve clichés of selling. II. Title

HF5438.25 .F367 2001
658.85—dc21   2001026989

Workman books are available at special discount when purchased in
bulk for premiums and sales promotions as well as for fund-raising or
educational use. Special editions or book excerpts can also be created
to specification. For details, contact the Special Sales Director at the
address below.

Workman Publishing Company, Inc.
708 Broadway
New York, NY 10003-9555

www.workman.com

Printed in the United States of America

First Printing October 2001
10 9 8 7 6 5 4 3 2 1

To my family,
who are the greatest gift in my life and the greatest teachers.
I've learned some of my best sales techniques from my children.

Acknowledgments

Talk about clichés. Being an optimist, I started this book project saying, "It'll be a piece of cake." This is one time when the cliché was proven wrong. Every project takes hard work and commitment. Circumstances took this book on a somewhat twisted path, and I could never have seen it through without the help and encouragement of some extraordinary people. I'd like to extend special thanks:

To Sally Kovalchick, whose work ethic and dedication were legendary. Her attention to detail was astounding. I was very sorry to see her pass on.

To Margot Herrera, who added strength and focus to every single page. She's someone who truly understands the concept of added value.

To Peter Workman, for understanding the vision of the book and giving it the go-ahead.

To all the people at Workman Publishing, who put their lives into every book.

To the many people who contributed their time and insights to help define the world of selling. Without them, this book would not have its eclectic value and wide-ranging appeal.

To my literary agent, Al Zuckerman, for his dedication and commitment on every project. In the world of agents, he is truly a rare breed.

Especially to Sharyn Kolberg, a special friend and partner who's made a huge difference in my life. She has a remarkable ability to take my ideas and make them sing. For a writer, that's a true talent. For me, that's a true gift.

CONTENTS

INTRODUCTION
That's Such *a* Cliché

Never take no for an answer. You get what you pay for. Attitude determines altitude. Knowledge is power. We've heard these sayings over and over again; we've repeated them over and over again. In fact, we've repeated them so often, we hardly pay attention to them anymore.

But here's the thing: Just because an expression is time-worn, just because it may be conventional wisdom or common knowledge, doesn't make it any less true or useful.

Isn't it just possible that clichés have more to offer than we may think?

What is a cliché, anyway? It's a common thought that has lost its impact through overuse. The world of sales is full of clichés. Why? Because they work! They've become clichés

> *"We are all salesmen every day of our lives. We are selling our ideas, our plans, our enthusiasms to those with whom we come in contact."*
>
> —CHARLES M. SCHWAB

because they're used every day. They've been put into action and proved to be true over and over again.

Secretary of State Colin Powell once said, "There are no secrets to success: Don't waste time looking for them. Success is the result of perfection, hard work, learning from failure, loyalty to those for whom you work, and persistence." The same sentiments apply to success in selling: It's the hard work and learning from failure; it's the persistence; it's applying the basics that have worked year in and year out that help ordinary salespeople achieve extraordinary success.

Other people might look at those achievers and say, "They were born lucky." "They have a special talent." "They got a great territory." The truth is, they simply exercised and implemented the basic truths of sales that always work. Those truths have become clichés.

Clichés don't come from statistical analysis of hard-core data. They're not based on the latest technological advances. Clichés come from the most basic truths of everyday experience. They develop from the tried and true, and from trial and error.

Because we hear these clichés so often, because they slip so easily off the tongue, we assume we have no more to learn from them. Not true.

One of the things you'll be hearing about throughout this book is the fact that I am studying the martial art Tae Kwon Do. In Tae Kwon Do, "forms" are one of the fundamentals in learning the art. Forms are composed of various strikes and blocks done in a particular sequence that you practice over and over again. You use these forms when you spar against opponents. You practice them so often that they become second nature to you. You constantly work to improve your forms so that they are at your command when you need them. And if at any point you get a bit careless or your technique begins to slip, you go back to the basic forms and rebuild your foundation.

That's what this book is about. The fundamentals of selling, the twelve clichés included in this book, are like the forms in Tae Kwon Do. They are the basic principles that serve as the groundwork for sales success. They cover the sales process from preparation to follow-through. They contain valuable lessons about organization, attitude, handling objections, selling value, persistence and tenacity, customer service, questioning, listening, and presentation techniques.

How can you be sure that these fundamental techniques work? Because this book is filled with advice and anecdotes from some of the top sales representatives and entrepreneurs around the country who live and prosper by these techniques. These salespeople represent dozens of different industries, from glass ornaments to computers, from beverages to pharmaceuticals, from lumber to coffee.

The criterion for interviewing people for this book was not what they sold, but that they were highly successful salespeople. The people you'll meet in these pages are commissioned salespeople, entrepreneurs, sales managers, marketing managers, regional managers, small business owners, franchise owners, and CEOs. They each have attained success by following many of the clichés included here, and have their own insights and stories to tell. They all have their own style and their own opinions to share.

The point is to provide you with knowledge culled from a wide variety of perceptions, experiences, industries, and sales cultures. Salespeople are always eager to hear how others achieved success, and, in the coming chapters, you'll read some great stories and gain valuable insights from the best of the best.

Some of the information here may appear to be just common sense. The problem is that common sense isn't so common anymore. That's why, when the same information comes from dozens of reliable sources, when the message is repeated over and over again about what the most successful salespeople do and what the least successful salespeople lack, perhaps it's time to go back and review the basics.

After all, nothing succeeds like success.

> *"People often ask me how I accomplished this or that. . . .*
>
> *I work hard; I set goals; I give customers service they don't expect. No one is ever shocked. Because, deep down, everyone knows that if they acted upon these 'clichés,' they'd be successful."*
>
> —DON FINK, VICE PRESIDENT,
> CITICORP PRIVATE BANK

[Come *with* *an* Empty Hand]

Success doesn't come from standing still or from doing the same things you've always done. My goal, in sales and in life, is to learn something new every day. Each day when I'm selling I ask myself, "What's the best way to do this, right here, right now?" I pull from all my resources and apply what I've learned over the years. That has helped me make the contents of this book more useful, more realistic, and more hands-on. Because I'm not speaking from theory; I'm speaking from experience.

I sell all day, every day. I sell my own services as a sales and management consultant, seminar leader, and keynote speaker. I run a literary agency through which I package and sell other people's books to publishers. As an author and radio and television host, I sell my own ideas and shows to publishers, advertisers, and media contacts. Simply put, I make my living by selling one thing or another every single day.

But it's amazing how much I still have to learn. I have successes, and I have my setbacks as well. I make mistakes every day. But my goal is constant improvement, because once you think you know how to sell, once you're convinced you're at the top of your game, that's when you get into trouble. That's when you start skipping over some of the fundamentals that made you successful in the first place.

My philosophy, and one of my favorite aphorisms, is "Once you think you're at the mountaintop, you stop climbing." Once you think you have all the answers, you stop reaching, you stop growing. This book is about how to keep climbing and how to make the climb fun, interesting, and rewarding.

When I first started training in the martial arts, a man whom I had not seen before joined our class. He was dressed in a white T-shirt and sweatpants. He was obviously not a beginner, and after the class ended, I discovered he was, in fact, a black belt. I asked him why he wasn't wearing it.

"If I come to this class wearing my black belt and thinking I know it all, I won't learn very much," he said. "To show my respect to the masters here, I come with an empty hand."

That is what I ask you to do with this book—to come with an empty hand. To know that you may have heard some of this before, but that you will hear it from a new perspective. To know that even a black belt comes to a beginners' class every once in a while to learn from a new master.

The masters who speak to you through these pages don't talk about any kind of sneaky closing techniques. They don't mention manipulation. They don't analyze their customers' personalities with psychological tests and then figure out how to sell to them.

Instead, they talk about tenacity, persistence, making good impressions, making plans and setting goals, selling added value, conscientious follow-through, and hours of hard work.

They talk about building relationships, living and working with passion, and selling with integrity.

And they do sometimes speak and act in clichés. But that's because these clichés have proved, time and again, to be crucial to every step we take toward success. These clichés hold more wisdom than you might imagine. I'm asking you to take a deeper look at them—there just might be more there than you think. I'm not reinventing the wheel here, although I may explain to you why the wheel works and maybe even how you can build a better one.

1 It Takes ALL Kinds

Suppose I asked you to paint a portrait of a typical salesperson. You couldn't do it. That's because every type of person goes into sales: men, women, old, young, funny, serious, calm, energetic. The cliché is that extroverted "people" people go into sales. But a test done by Bob Means, president and founder of Oxycon (a recruitment firm), showed that introverts make just as successful salespeople as extroverts, perhaps because introverts are such good listeners.

"The good in you is like the water in a well. The more you draw from it, the more fresh water will seep in. If you do not draw from it, the water will only become stagnant."

—DENG MING-DAO,
365 TAO: DAILY MEDITATIONS

Every type of person has the potential to be successful in this sometimes difficult but often extremely rewarding field. Why is it, then, that some salespeople live up to that potential while others do not?

As you read through this book, you'll meet all kinds of successful salespeople from different industries and a variety of backgrounds. They have very different personalities. Most have many years' experience in sales; many have worked their way up in their companies and are now managers, vice presidents, and CEOs. Whether or not they're still out selling, these are people who have earned their success the hard way—they've worked for it.

So what makes these people different from the thousands who enter the world of sales each year and are *not* successful? What made it possible for them to keep going through the tough times, rejections, and failures? Following are some of the key things these high-achieving salespeople have done, each in his or her own way, to make it to the top and stay there.

Foster *the* Right Attitude

If one could achieve success easily, it wouldn't have the same meaning. There wouldn't have been thousands of books written about it over the years. All of us get hit with difficulties every day, and we have to find ways to deal with them. It's our attitude toward these obstacles that makes the difference.

Look at the people we hold up as achievers: CEOs, millionaires, celebrities. It may appear that they all lead charmed lives. A few of them may seem blessed. But eventually we find out that even the blessed face the trials and tribulations of life. We learn, for instance, that Albert Einstein failed algebra in high school, that Olympic gold medal winner Bruce Jenner was dyslexic, that Dave Thomas of Wendy's grew up in unhappy foster homes.

But they didn't let their hardships defeat them. They all worked hard to overcome obstacles, to become better people, and to achieve success. They turned their lives around by not giving in to circumstance. You can dwell on your limitations or you can say, "I may not have been born with anything special, but I'm going to build something special nonetheless. I will build it through effort and attitude." And if you build it right, it will give you a great edge against the people who were born with more than you. They may take their success for granted. They can't possibly appreciate success as much as someone who has worked so hard for it.

> *"Don't bother about genius. Don't worry about being clever. Trust in hard work, perseverance, and determination."*
>
> —*FREDERICK TREVES*

[Watch Out *for* Naysayers]

A businessman bought a paper at the same newsstand every morning. Every morning, he gave the vendor a huge smile and a friendly hello. And, every morning, the vendor ignored him. One day, a colleague (who watched this ritual unfold almost every day) asked, "Why do you continue to give this guy such a friendly greeting? He never even talks to you."

The man replied, "I'm not going to let that individual determine how I act for the day."

Every day, your attitude is challenged by other people and by outside events. How will you react? Will you let adversity or obstacles stop you from moving forward? Or will you look at the situation objectively and find the lesson that can be learned or the action that can be taken to turn things around? Will you let a negative person influence your day, your life? Or will you remember the words of Eleanor Roosevelt, who said, "No one can make you feel inferior without your consent."

A few years ago, Alice Braden, CEO of Braden Business Information, Inc., left her salaried position and opened a business of her own. During the transition period, she met many people she refers to as "naysayers."

"Naysayers are people who either don't believe in you or put you down for trying," says Braden. "They either look at you warily and say, 'Oh, isn't that nice,' or they say, 'I had a friend who started her own business and she went under in a year.' One of the best ways I've found to deal with naysayers is to simply say to myself, 'Thank you for sharing.' That's their opinion and their perspective. I don't have to make it mine."

[Turn Rejection
into an Asset]

Some successful salespeople, like Donald Fink, a vice president at Citicorp Private Bank, turn discouragement into motivation. Fink is one of the most driven and dedicated people you could ever meet. Besides being a high-powered executive, he finished second in his age group in the 1998 Hawaii Ironman World Championship.

"I was a kid who always had big ideas," says Fink. "But my parents were content with being average. They were always telling me, 'Don't push yourself so hard. Take it easy on yourself.' What that said to me, even though I didn't realize it at the time, is that the people I love best in the world are basically telling me I'm not good enough to achieve my goals. That was a very powerful motivator for me to prove them wrong."

For Don Fink, negativity is an unlimited fuel. "I tap into it all the time," he says. "I am motivated by many things, including money and recognition. But I am most motivated by the people who are convinced of my inabilities or the impossibility of achieving my goals. Those people, who used to get me depressed, now get me energized. They are fuel to my fire."

You can't buy into other people's versions of your life. When they say, "This is too hard; you'll never do it," what they really mean is that it's too hard for *them.* They could never do it, so

> *"The human spirit is never finished when it is defeated. . . . It is finished when it surrenders."*
>
> —BEN STEIN

they assume you won't be able to do it either (perhaps they even secretly hope you won't). If you buy into their reasoning, it means you're going to cheat yourself out of your goals.

I too have experienced my share of rejections and obstacles in my life. I've been canceled, I've been terminated, I've been turned down and turned away. But each time it happens, I ask myself three questions:

- "Who is this person who is evaluating me? Is he credible?"
- "Does this person know my true capabilities?"
- "So you think I can't do this? I'll show you that I can!"

Like Frank, I find there's nothing like someone telling me "no" to push me forward. I channel the rejection in a positive way, and then success is the greatest revenge. It's not rejection that counts, but what you do with it. It's the ability to take that information and say, "These people may have had their reasons, but that doesn't mean they're right. They rejected me, so let me figure out what I can do differently next time. I'm going to learn from this and move on. But I'm never going to let those people determine my success."

This, of course, is easier to say than do. But if you're a salesperson, you have to accept that it's part of your life. It doesn't matter whether or not you're just beginning or if you're one of the best; it still comes—literally—with the territory.

[Build Strong Relationships]

All successful salespeople recognize this one simple truth: Most of the business we do is based upon the relationships we have with our customers. It stands to reason, then, that our best customers will be those with whom we have the best relationships. But how do you build those relationships?

People may agree to see you or speak with you because of the company or product you represent, but in the end, they buy because of who you are and how you treat them. They'll do business with you if:

❑ **They like you.** This means that customers find you agreeable to deal with and take pleasure in your company. It doesn't mean you have to become best friends with every prospect or customer, or that you necessarily become part of their lives outside of work (although in some cases you might). It means that within the context of buyer/seller interactions, customers know you to be affable, respectful, considerate, and accommodating.

❑ **They have trust in you.** They rely on your integrity. They know that you're concerned for their best interest (as well as your own—they know you're there to sell them something). This is a trust that you earn as you go, from your initial meeting through the closing of the sale, customer service, and follow-through.

❑ **They respect you.** They consider you an expert in your field, and they esteem you as a peer and a colleague who has a thorough knowledge of their company and industry.

These three factors work together to give you an edge. Prospects won't even consider giving you business based solely on the fact that they like you; they give you business because they like you *and* they trust and respect you. You have to prove yourself worthy. If you simply depend on the fact that you're a nice person, you won't get very far.

[Earn Your Customers' Trust]

Of the above three elements in your relationship with your customers—them liking you, trusting you, and respecting you—trust is the most important. Trust is something you earn by showing customers that you have their bottom line in mind as well as your own. Trust is made up of:

- **Truth.** Customers expect you to be honest about your product or service. They trust that if your product or service is not right for them, you will let them know. If you do, they will gladly call you again when they need your product.

- **Reliability.** Customers want to know that you will be there when they need you, and that if you make promises, you will keep them.

- **Understanding.** Do you understand your customers' needs? Have you spent time getting to know what their goals are and what they want to accomplish?

- **Service.** What do you do to differentiate yourself? Do you provide added value and deliver more than is expected?

- **Truth.** Again, from beginning to end, customers depend on your honesty.

David D'Alessandro, CEO of John Hancock Financial Services and author of *Brand Warfare,* feels that too many salespeople rely on their company's reputation rather than their own to make the sale. "The fact that John Hancock has a good reputation is only as good as the person who's representing us," he says. "Our customers don't shake hands with our building. They get to know a salesperson who comes into their living room.

"Look at what we do for a living. We sell life insurance. This is a product that produces no benefits for the people who actually make the purchase. The benefits go to their relatives after they're gone. They have to trust that they're buying the right product from the right company. I believe strongly that a company or brand name gets a salesperson in the door. That's about all. It's the salesperson's own reputation that in the end is much more important than the company he or she represents.

"What you need to do is build your own personal brand within your customer base so that people don't think of your company first, they think of you. Our customers tell us, 'I don't know John Hancock. I know my salesperson, Joe Smith. If Joe Smith tells me something is going to get done, I trust his word.' And that's how sales are made."

> *"The toughest thing about the power of trust is that it's very difficult to build and very easy to destroy."*
>
> —THOMAS J. WATSON, SR.

[Trust Yourself]

Trust yourself. Sounds so simple, but in the face of the continual rejection that comes with choosing sales as a field, it can be the hardest thing of all.

I recently learned (or relearned) this lesson myself. I had been speaking with a prospect for several weeks, and everything seemed to be going along fine. We had many positive conversations, and then . . . nothing. I called and got no response. I called again. Again no return call. That's when the voice in my head (you know that voice; you have one too) started tormenting me. What did I do wrong? What did I say in the last conversation that had offended him so? Was my proposal so off base that he didn't even want to speak with me again?

Finally, after two and a half weeks, I got him on the phone. He apologized for not calling me back. He was out of the office, he said, because his mother had passed away suddenly. This was a graphic reminder not to listen to that voice that tells me I'm not good enough. If you don't believe you're good, your attitude is easily infected by outside circumstances, as well as your own self-doubts.

Comedian Bill Cosby once said that he didn't know the secret to success, but that the secret to failure was trying to please everyone. You don't have to be the perfect salesperson. Prospects aren't looking for perfection, they're looking for human connections. They're looking to form relationships with real people who are serious about business but who don't take themselves so seriously. Prospects are buying you as much as they are your product or service, so your best bet is to connect with them on a personal level by relaxing and just being yourself.

Being a successful salesperson means knowing your business and believing in what you do. It doesn't mean giving up your personality or your sense of humor to follow someone else's style. It doesn't mean trying to become something you're not. It means building on your best qualities and having faith in your own abilities.

You are the only one who can truly determine your success. If you have doubts about what you're doing, if you don't believe in what you're selling, those doubts will resonate in your voice, in your actions (or lack of them), and in your overall sales efforts. It's not a lack of technique that will hold you back—it's that little voice in your head that says, "Give up. You'll never get this sale."

To keep that little voice at bay, be choosy about the company you keep—don't associate with people who have a bad attitude. Read books about individuals and organizations that have kept going when people told them something couldn't be done. Talk to people you trust, people who believe in you and can offer advice and encouragement. Keep educating yourself so that you gain new skills and sharpen the ones you have.

Once you silence that negative voice and replace it with the right attitude, failure is no longer an option. Out of all the ingredients I could list that go into making a successful salesperson, the final ingredient, the one that can come from only one source, is you. Successful salespeople pick and choose the tools and techniques that best suit their own styles and personalities. They don't let other people convince them that *their* way is the only way to go. At the end of the day, they trust themselves.

CHAPTER RECAP:
IT TAKES ALL KINDS

[*What does it take to be a successful salesperson?*]

Build the right attitude.
- Don't let hardships defeat you.
- Don't let your circumstances define you.

Watch out for naysayers.
- Use others' negativity as fuel for your own motivation.
- Don't buy into other people's versions of your life and cheat yourself out of your goals.

Turn rejection into an asset.
- If you experience rejection, ask yourself:
  1. "What is the credibility of the person evaluating me?"
  2. "What does this person know about my true capabilities?"
  3. "How can I channel my anger about this rejection into positive action?"
- Don't take rejection personally, as an insult to who you are.
- Do take rejection personally as a chance to get feedback and learn from your mistakes.

Build the right relationships.

- People do business with you if:
  - They like you.
  - They trust you.
  - They respect you.

Earn customers' trust.

- Show customers that you have their bottom line in mind as well as your own.
- Keep in mind the TRUST acronym:
  Truth
  Reliability
  Understanding
  Service
  Truth
- Build your own personal brand within your customer base so that people think of you first, then of your company.

Trust yourself.

- Take your commitment to your job seriously.
- Keep educating yourself to gain new skills and sharpen the ones you already have.

2 Never Take No *for an* Answer

If you want to know what "never take no for an answer" really means, you should meet advertising legend Anthony Wainwright, vice chairman of McKinney and Silver in Raleigh, North Carolina. Persistence ought to be his middle name. He's willing to spend years developing a sale.

Here's a case in point. While Wainwright was working on the Stroh's beer advertising account, he became friendly with Jim Buell, Stroh's marketing director. When Buell left Stroh's to become director of new products for Anheuser-Busch,

> *"Our greatest weakness lies in giving up. The most certain way to succeed is to always try just one more time."*
>
> —THOMAS EDISON

Wainwright called him and even went to visit him at the company's headquarters in St. Louis. Buell was very gracious but told Wainwright he didn't have anything for him. "Anyone who knows me will tell you that I often describe myself as the 'last man standing,'" says Wainwright. "I always hang in when everyone else has left and gone home. When I go after something, I'm persistent as can be."

Almost every week, Wainwright would drop Buell a note. Wainwright explains: "The trick is to go in with an idea that is directly related to the prospect's business. Even if your idea is not accepted, it shows the prospect you're thinking of him and his business. It puts you in a different category from your competition. I'd say things like 'Have you thought about this kind of acquisition?' Or I'd write, 'Have you considered an extension of this line of products or perhaps a different method of distribution?' Then every few months, I'd get on a plane and fly to St. Louis. We'd have lunch and Buell would say, 'Sorry, Tony, but I have nothing for you right now.' So I'd go back and start writing notes all over again."

The cycle continued for seven years. (Of course, Buell wasn't the only client Wainwright was pursuing at the time. Then, as now, Wainwright wrote at least fifty letters every day, even on Saturdays and Sundays.) At the end of the seventh year, Wainwright finally got a call from Buell, asking him to come to Busch headquarters. That's when he said, "We're introducing several new brands—and we want you to do the advertising."

The result? Almost $30 million a year for Wainwright's company.

"So now I preach to anyone who will listen," says Wainwright. "I tell them, never give up. If a deal doesn't work out, I still don't give up. I say to myself, 'Okay, that didn't work out. But who knows what will happen in the next seven years?'"

What Part *of* "No" Don't You Understand?

Most people see no as a rejection or a dismissal. Successful salespeople see no as a challenge, more of a postponement than a refusal. Loosely translated into salespeak, "no" should simply mean "not now," or "not yet," or "not this one."

It may be that "Never take no for an answer" describes what people used to think of as the cliché salesperson: the pushy individual determined to make a sale at all costs, with no consideration for a customer's needs or wants. That's not what it means now. It's about being persistent, not pushy. It means that you keep on going, like the Energizer bunny, until someone finally takes notice. It's about exploring all avenues to a sale, being creative in your approaches, and being professionally tenacious. If you see value in your product or service for a particular customer, you will find ways to keep returning with additional information until the customer understands that value as well.

If you do not see the value for that particular customer, then you will move on and keep making cold calls until you *do* find the most qualified customers.

Ask any successful corporate executive, "Why did you let that sales rep in the door when you turned away so many others?" He or she will probably answer, "Because that person kept calling me with useful information. He was always there with ideas to help me move forward, whether it was a suggestion about business or about my personal interests. Finally, he ended up calling on the day I needed something, and he got the business."

[Getting Past *the* Gatekeeper]

The greatest barrier salespeople ever face is getting a foot in the door. Many salespeople get stopped before they even reach the decision-maker (the person who has the authority to buy your service or product). They get stopped by the person known as the "gatekeeper," the one who holds the key for you to get in the decision-maker's door. A gatekeeper can be a public relations person who sets up all the decision-maker's meetings. It can be someone you know who might be able to introduce you to the decision-maker. The company's receptionist can be a gate-keeper. Usually, however, the gatekeeper is the decision-maker's assistant, and it is his or her job to screen calls (and get rid of annoying salespeople).

Remember that gatekeepers are human beings who are just trying to do their job. Too many salespeople see them merely as barriers to be breached and treat them accordingly. This attitude will get you nowhere. Sometimes, in order to storm the castle, the most useful weapon you have is a friend at the gate.

Here are some ways to get through a tough screener.

1. Form a relationship with the gatekeeper.

Give the gatekeeper the same respect you would give to the CEO. Not only is it the right thing to do, but you also never know how much power that person has. If you can make the gatekeeper your friend, you may succeed where others have failed because he or she has three things to offer:

- ❑ **Inside information.** Many decision-makers spend more time with their assistants than they do with their families! If you can get the assistant's trust, it's going to be much easier to make him or her your ally. One way to do this is to ask for the assistant's help. For example, you might ask a gatekeeper for insights and ideas about how to do your job more efficiently without wasting anyone's time.

  Recently, I showed up for an appointment with a high-level executive at a major television network and was informed that he'd be a few minutes late. Chatting with his assistant, I explained that this meeting was important to me and asked if she could tell me anything about her boss that might help me—anything about his personality, his hobbies, his likes, his dislikes.

She told me he was a straight shooter—that he was very direct and straightforward—and liked people who were that way with him. She also told me he was a big Mets fan. The meeting was successful, largely because these two pieces of information gave me a better idea of what to expect and some insight on how to relate to this man when we met.

❏ **Hidden power.** You never know how much power the gatekeeper really has—not authority to buy your product or service, but the power to influence the decision-maker's decisions. It's not unusual for a decision-maker to come out of a meeting and ask the gatekeeper, "So what did you think of Bob Smith?" If the gatekeeper says, "He was very rude on the phone" or "It took him three weeks to send us the material we requested," the impression you made on the gatekeeper may outweigh the impression you made on the boss. Too many salespeople underestimate the unseen or untitled authority gatekeepers possess.

❏ **The ability to spread the word.** Don't forget that gatekeepers are often great networkers. They usually have contacts throughout the company and can be very useful in promoting you to another executive or department. And if they leave the company and become a gatekeeper for another company's decision-maker, when the new decision-maker is looking for your type of product or service, the gatekeeper will likely say, "When I was at Acme General, we used Bob Smith and were very happy with his services," giving you an in with the new boss.

2. Use praise and recognition.

Many salespeople fail to recognize gatekeepers as individuals, but it can make the difference between getting your foot in the door and getting the boot. After my meeting with the network executive, I sent a thank-you note to his assistant, acknowledging her help and praising the positive attitude she displayed every time I called. The next time I spoke to her, she told me how much she appreciated my note and that she had shown it to her boss.

As soon as I get off the phone with a gatekeeper who has given me information, I call the company back and speak to the receptionist. I get the full name (and correct spelling) of the individual with whom I was just speaking. I don't ask the gatekeeper directly because I want my note to be a surprise.

I often send a card that shows a picture of a clock on the outside, with the words "Time. Your most valuable commodity." Inside, it says, "Thanks for sharing some of it with me." I handwrite a line or two: "Thanks again for your time on the phone.

I really appreciate your help regarding . . ." Then I insert my business card and mail it off immediately.

Of course, you can simply send a handwritten note or make your own card on the computer. The point is to acknowledge the help you were given and to separate yourself from the rest of the pack. This shows gatekeepers and/or prospects, before you even meet them, that you're willing to go that little extra step most people don't even think about.

[Getting *to the* Decision-Maker]

Suppose you manage to get past the gatekeeper. If you're lucky, you'll be able to speak to the decision-maker right then; most of the time, however, the person in authority is in a meeting, out in the field, or out of town. So you'll have to energize that bunny once again and get ready for round two of "Never take no": getting through to the decision-maker.

1. Send a positive message through voice mail.

Some salespeople leave mysterious, even misleading messages on voice mail just to get prospects to call them back. They'll say something like "Hi, this is Bob Smith at 555-1234. . . . I have something important to talk to you about. . . ." Then they concoct a false static sound to make it sound as if the call has been cut off. They figure that once they have the prospect on the phone, they can rope him into a sale (or at least an appointment). That might work once or twice. But most decision-makers are extremely savvy and have heard every trick in the book. You're much better off being brief and straightforward.

If you've never spoken to the person before, don't just say what your product is; include a benefit in your message. For instance, instead of saying, "Hello, this is Jennifer Adams and I'm calling with regard to training programs for your company," you might say, "Hello. This is Jennifer Adams. I'm calling regarding some ideas I have for improving your company's sales performance." Then you would say, "You can reach me at 555-1234. I'll be in on Thursday morning. If I don't hear from you then, I'll call you back in the afternoon." That way, you're inviting the decision-maker to call you back and at the same time leaving open the possibility that you'll call again.

2. Never take a no from a person who can't say yes.

If you're going to get a no, make sure it's from someone who actually has the authority to make that decision. If you're not sure who that person is, start at the top. Call the office of the president. Even if you don't get through, you'll probably speak to his or her assistant, who, as discussed earlier, can give you invaluable feedback on the structure and inner workings of the company.

Ask the assistant to direct you to the person who handles the purchase of your type of product or service. When the assistant says, "David Clarke handles that," you can call David Clarke and say that you've just been speaking with the president's office and it was recommended that you talk with him. You can use this sometimes winding path for two purposes: to get information that will help you learn more about the account, and to build relationships all along the line.

If selling to the top doesn't work out, you might try going in another direction. Go to the people in the field or the sales support staff. Tell them you're trying to get some information about their company or about the particular products they sell (salespeople love to talk about their products). They, too, may be able to provide you with information you can use to become an expert on that organization. Then, when you do get through to the top decision-maker, you'll have a strong foundation for suggestions on how your product or service can benefit the entire organization.

3. When the straightforward route fails ...

When you've done your homework, called several times, left a number of voice mail and e-mail messages, sent two or three creative cards, and you *still* get no response, you may want to try something "out of the box."

Harrison Fisher, a vice president within Small Business Services, Chase Manhattan Bank, uses what he calls the "one foot in the door" technique. After he's spoken to a prospect once and can't get back in touch, he sends a stretchy foam ball in the shape of a foot. He puts his business card in between the first and second toes with a note that says, "Now that I've got one foot in the door, how do I get my other foot in and show you the value of our products and services?" Another successful salesperson uses the same technique, except that she sends a miniature shoe on a key chain along with her note. She told me she gets an 88 percent response to this.

There's another technique that can work extremely well when you've been persistent over a long period of time. It's called "If I can speak to God . . ." You use this after you've called and faxed and Fed Exed and voice-mailed and done everything else you can think of. In other words, you must earn the right to leave this message (either with an assistant or on voice mail): "Every night before I go to sleep I speak to God. Why can't I talk to you?"

There are three reasons for leaving this message: First, to stand out from all the other voice mail this prospect gets. Some executives get fifty to one hundred messages a day. If you don't get their attention, they'll listen for about ten seconds and then erase the message. Second, if you've been persistent and done all the work previous to this, that message will make a great impact. Third, if you can leave the message with an assistant who is your ally, it can have the greatest impact of all. I have gotten callbacks from billionaires and notoriously hard-to-reach Hollywood agents using this method.

You never know when humor will pay off. Dennis Holt is chairman of Western International Media, one of the largest advertising sales companies in California. Several years ago, he pursued a particularly resistant prospect who never returned his phone calls. When Holt finally got him on the phone, the man said bluntly, "Look. I'm not going to do business with you, so don't bother me anymore." Trying to keep the conversation light, Holt replied, "I guess I can count you as a 'firm maybe' then?" The prospect failed to see the humor in this and hung up. However, he called Holt back two days later. "I told some of my friends what you said about counting me as a 'firm maybe,'" he said. "They all thought it was very funny. I realized they were right, and I think we ought to talk about working together."

Sometimes it pays to go out on a limb. Tony Wainwright once sat in the reception room of the William Wrigley, Jr., Co. (of Wrigley's gum fame) for two days, trying to get a meeting with company chairman Philip K. Wrigley. Finally, he cornered a window washer, gave him $200, and got him to write on the chairman's window: "Wainwright has a great idea." Naturally, Wrigley came out immediately to see who this Wainwright fellow was and to hear what he had to say.

Another bold move got Wainwright in to see a famous children's products entrepreneur. He composed a little song, asked ten of his daughter's young friends to dress up in costumes, and took them into the company's reception room. When the entrepreneur walked through the room, Wainwright had the girls sing his song. The entrepreneur was highly amused, and Wainwright got the business.

These may be extreme examples, but the point is to make

an impression. You have to follow up with solid ideas and service, but using a unique approach can get you in the door. You don't necessarily have to be outrageous, or spend a lot of money on color and splash—just be creative and use what you know about the person you're pursuing.

[Persistent, Not Pushy]

Some salespeople, especially those who are just beginning their careers, run into problems because they don't know the difference between pushiness and persistence. I've heard numerous complaints over the years from customers who felt that salespeople tend to be too aggressive. The salespeople they had in mind called ten times a week just to ask, "Are you ready to buy yet?"

Successful salespeople are assertive, not aggressive. They're persistent in a manner that is not overbearing. Potential customers know it's your job to sell them something; you're not trying to fool them into making a purchase. You're trying to help your prospects solve their problems; you're not trying to persuade them to do something they don't want to do.

Stanley Kravitz, a division vice president of the Metropolitan employment agency in New York City, contacts prospects often enough so that they remember his company, but not so often that it becomes offensive. He uses what he calls a series of "drips," letters sent out to prospects designed to keep Metropolitan in mind.

"I deal with human resources executives of large companies," says Kravitz. "They probably get twenty to thirty calls a day from people in my industry. So I send an introductory letter and follow it with a phone call. Then, depending on what happens with the call, I send another short letter, no more than two or three paragraphs. I know they don't have a lot of time to read, but occasionally I'll include an insert or some article of interest. I try to make the letters interesting and creative. I don't want to become intrusive by calling them every day, but I do keep in touch often enough so that I'm in their minds."

When you're pursuing business over a long period of time, it helps to keep track of how many calls you've made and the messages you've left. That can be done with computer software, such as ACT! or GoldMine, or simply on three-by-five index cards. Include the contact's name and phone number, the date of each call you make, and, if you get through, the key points that were covered in each call. Not only will that help you keep track, but also, when you look back and see that it was the fifteenth call that finally got through, it serves as a reminder that persistence really does pay off.

"Patience and tenacity of purpose are worth more than twice their weight in cleverness."

—THOMAS HENRY HUXLEY

It pays off for everyone, whether the person trying to make the sale is a first-time rookie or the head of a multi-million-dollar company. Mo Siegel, now vice chairman of the Hain Celestial Group, describes how his former company, Celestial Seasonings, the largest manufacturer of herb tea in North America, merged with the Hain Food Group.

"Irwin Simon, the CEO of Hain, kept bugging me to meet with him about the idea of merging his company, Hain Food Group, with Celestial Seasonings.

"He'd call every few weeks and give me one more reason it would be a good idea for our companies to merge. He was incredibly persistent. Finally, he gave me so many reasons I agreed to sit down and have a hard-core conversation about it. Once he got me to have that conversation, we were both doggedly tenacious about seeing the deal through and making it happen."

Of course, Irwin Simon, being the CEO of a large company, didn't have to get past a gatekeeper to gain access to Mo Siegel; nor does Mo Siegel have to worry about being able to get through to heads of companies. But even when he was just starting out, Siegel found the way to get people on the phone.

"I just go directly to the person I want to speak to—and persist," he says. "Or I find a friend or someone who can give me a referral to the person I want to speak to. I'm never afraid to pick up the phone and call. Some people say that they're reticent about making calls. But when you talk to the really successful people in the world, they're not afraid to do it. If you want to be a salesperson, it's the price of entry."

[Your Foot's *in the* Door— Don't Give Up Now!]

Your foot is in the door; you've gotten an appointment with the decision-maker. Now is a time when you definitely can't take no for an answer. Now it's time to turn a prospect into a customer.

Just because the prospect has finally agreed to let you in the door doesn't mean the sale is closed. Some decision-makers give in simply because you've been so persistent. They may be seeing you as a favor to someone who referred you. They may be interested in your product, but not necessarily ready to buy. So now it's up to you to make sure that the prospect understands exactly how your product or service will benefit his or her company.

"Never take no for an answer" is a driving mechanism that forces you to move forward and come up with new strategies to get the business. "Never take no for an answer" is more than just blindly pushing a product. It is having a clear understanding of the customer's needs. All successful salespeople stress the fact that they must do their jobs—and do them well—if they expect to get a yes. They understand that they must give prospects enough information about their products, and they must be sure their products meet their customers' needs.

This is a lesson that Stanley Mason learned early in his sales career. Mason holds more than sixty-five patents for his consumer product inventions and has been called a modern-day Thomas Edison. He sells other people's inventions as well as his own. A friend of his developed a special kind of bookbinding glue that would turn transparent when applied, and Mason decided that it would be perfect for schools and libraries. He traveled around trying to sell this glue, and when he met with a school superintendent in Pennsylvania who didn't want to buy it, he was furious. He went out to his car, slammed the door shut, and fumed. But then he thought, "Why am I furious with the superintendent? I should be furious with myself. The customer said no and I wasn't ready for it. I didn't give him enough information to understand why he should buy my glue. It was my fault, not his."

That has continued to be Mason's philosophy. When he gets a no from a prospect, he believes the prospect is really saying, "I don't yet have the information I need to say yes."

[Hanging In *over the* Long Haul]

There are times when it becomes difficult to remain persistent, especially when a sale extends over a long period. You may even be tempted to give up and walk away. However, if that temptation should arise, take a lesson from Nancy Nape, national account manager for Knoll, Inc., furniture manufacturers.

One of Knoll's specialties is manufacturing upscale office systems (cubicles) for large businesses. Several years ago, a large multinational bank was constructing a new building in midtown Manhattan and was considering Knoll's products as well as its major competitor's.

One of the design features of Knoll's product was a four-inch-high raceway base, a passageway built to accommodate electrical and computer cables at the base of the cubicle walls. The competitor's product had a small raceway at the bottom of the cubicle wall and another small one at the top. The competitor claimed that their product was superior, since running both types of cable together would cause cross-conductivity. In other words, the electrical wires would interfere with the computer lines.

The bank's senior vice president liked the look and the flexibility of Knoll's product, but was scared off by the warnings from its competitor. Nancy Nape, however, wouldn't take no for an answer. She asked the VP, "If we can prove to you that cross-conductivity will not be a problem, will you go ahead and order our product?" The VP agreed, but Nape still had to convince the head of Management Information Systems (MIS), who was in charge of the new building's technology. She kept calling and calling, and the MIS director kept refusing to meet with her. Finally, he explained that MIS was installing state-of-the-art high-speed equipment in the new building and didn't want to have any problems down the road.

Again, Nape asked, "If we can prove to you that cross-conductivity will not be a problem, will you go ahead and order our product?" The MIS director reluctantly agreed, although he said he didn't know how that could be accomplished. Nape wasn't sure either, but she wasn't about to give up. First, she had to convince her company that the cost and time of testing would be worthwhile. Then she had to find someone who would test the wiring. She contacted Bell Labs, the company that was supplying the cables to the new bank building, and convinced them that the testing would be to their benefit as well. After all, if their cables didn't work in close proximity to each other, they would have difficulty installing them for other clients as well.

At last, Nape was able to convince all parties to test the wiring. They taped the two wiring systems together, ran data at the same high speeds the bank would use, and plugged in a wide variety of electrical appliances. There was no cross-conductivity. Bell Labs sent a letter to the MIS director at the bank, and the sale went through—more than a year after Nape's first contact.

For an entire year, Nape would not accept the word *no*. She had to convince two different people at the bank, the higher-ups at her own company, and the testers at Bell Labs. But her persistence paid off, and the bank became a long-term customer of the company.

[Handling Objections]

"It costs too much." "We already have a supplier for that." "We don't need your service right now—maybe sometime in the future." When you hear objections like these, remember what Stanley Mason said: The prospect is saying no because you haven't presented him with enough information to say yes. You haven't yet found a satisfactory match between the benefits of your product or service and the prospect's needs or desires.

Before you meet your prospect, write down the three strongest reasons he or she should do business with you and your company ("Our product is 20 percent stronger than our competitor's," or "We have the largest customer support department in the industry," or "Using our service can save you up to $100,000 a year in production costs"). If you are faced with an objection, you have the key benefits at your fingertips.

Objections create opportunities for you to understand the prospect. If a prospect says, "I already have a supplier for that," ask questions. Find out who the supplier is and whether or not the prospect is happy with that supplier. If the answer is yes, find out why. Maybe there are ways that your product or service can make this prospect even happier.

Your goal is to present your value to the prospect. What makes your product or service unique? What is the one thing you are able to do that your competition cannot? That's what prospects really want to know when they bring up objections.

For instance, you might hear a typical objection like "I don't have the money in the budget" or "I'm happy with our present vendor." The worst thing you can do is argue with a prospect when an objection comes up. As soon as you argue, you lose. The prospect will immediately get defensive and will not listen to what you have to say. Let

"Man may remove all obstacles through quiet perseverance."

—CHINESE PROVERB

the prospect know you're sympathetic to his or her position (remember, you get more with honey than with vinegar).

You can often diffuse an objection by using the three-step "feel-felt-found" method. Empathize with your prospect by saying, "I understand how you *feel*." Then build on the success you've had with other customers by saying, "Many of my present customers *felt* the same way. But when they *found* out how much time they saved using our product [or service], they were amazed. I'd like to find out if we can do the same for you." Finish by saying, "I'll be in your area Thursday morning and Friday afternoon. Which is better for you?"

This method is itself a cliché because it's been used successfully so many times. But it doesn't work when you do it by rote. You have to know your benefits inside and out. You have to practice the technique until you can put it into your own words and let it come out naturally.

Needless to say, the feel-felt-found method doesn't work for every objection. For instance, people who are very busy will tell you they just don't have time to see you. I discovered a successful method for handling this objection during a phone call with an editor at one of the largest publishing companies in New York. He's worked on some of the all-time best-selling books, and he's very tough to get in to see. Although he took my phone call, he said several times that he was too busy to fit me into his schedule.

Finally, I said, "I'll tell you what. Give me just fifteen minutes of your time, and if I can't show something of tremendous value to your company, I'll never call you again."

"Never?"

"Never."

"You're on," he said. We had our meeting, and he ended up spending almost forty-five minutes with me.

I've used this method several times since then, and it usually works. You have to live up to your word, however, and give up on the prospect who doesn't find your product or service of value within the fifteen-minute time slot.

When "Never Take No . . ." Doesn't Apply

Of course, there's at least one exception to every rule—and every cliché.

"Never take no for an answer" makes sense most of the time.

But on occasion, salespeople themselves have to say no to a prospect. This may mean losing business in the present, but often it means more business in the future.

Below are five key reasons for saying no to a sale.

1. The sale goes against your goals and priorities.

Will the sale move you and your company forward toward the goals you've set up? If so, go after it. But if the return on investment isn't there, if there are other prospects who would be a better match, then it's time to say no.

"Every organization has to have checks and balances to ensure that a prospect doesn't become a customer at a loss to the organization and at a loss to the individual who made the sale," says Larry Frank, executive vice president of ComDoc, a document solutions company (copiers, faxes, networking systems, etc.). Not long ago, Frank was accompanying an inexperienced salesperson to a meeting with a prospect. The salesperson had met with this prospect before and had offered a pricing plan. "I realized that he had offered way too deep a discount," says Frank. "The sales rep and his manager had all sorts of rationalizations as to why they had offered that discount, but it didn't make sense for our company. We were getting locked into a five-year contract where we would lose money. I had to explain this to the customer and back out of the sale."

If the pursuit of a particular sale requires a large concentration of effort that will take you away from higher priorities, then it's time to say no. If the value is not there for you, it's not likely to be there for your customer, either. You might think that in every case, your highest priority is to make the sale. But if you do your research and find out about the prospect before the sales process gets too far along, you might realize that this just doesn't fit in with your sales goals. When that happens, it's a good idea to walk away.

2. You can't deliver.

The problem may be an issue of time, or it could be the specifications of the product the customer wants. You could try to push the sale through anyway and hope that you can deliver what you promise—but if you can't, you've lost a customer for life. And if you can't make the delivery, the negative word of mouth will prevent you from making sales to many other prospects as well. If you know you can't give the customer what he or she needs, just say so and move on.

3. You don't like dealing with the customer.

Some customers are downright rude and disrespectful. Others may run their business in an unethical manner and expect you to do the same (for instance, they may want you to give them kickbacks). Still others are unrealistically demanding, wanting services that no one could possibly provide. If the sale at hand is the only one on the horizon, you may feel you have to put up with the abuse. But when you have enough going on, you don't have to take business that you know will produce more headaches than revenue. You must make a realistic evaluation of the cost of doing business with a high-maintenance customer. If someone demands constant attention and a huge amount of work for very little return, you won't be able to spend quality time with other customers who may be bringing in a higher profit.

There are customers who are constantly asking you to do things for them, like "throw in" extra parts or supplies for free, or they want you to give them more of a discount. These customers are just not worth the aggravation. If they cannot see the value of your product or service, it's time for you to say no.

Leaving the customer is not a negative in this case; it only shows how much you value your time and product. And don't think that just because you drop a customer you'll never hear from him or her again. There are times when customers you decided were not worth the effort will come back to you. This usually happens after they've tried other vendors who could not give them the quality that you could provide.

4. *The customer is better off with another vendor.*
Nobody ever wants to admit that the competition might do a better job. Sometimes, however, they might have a different setup or be able to meet a particular customer's production demands better than your company can. It simply may be a better match for your prospect to go with someone else. As long as you have other prospects and customers to go to, this is an easy no. Tell your prospect, "After listening to your goals and challenges, I realize that the product we sell isn't quite what you

need. I recommend you try XYZ Company." Guaranteed, that prospect will appreciate your honesty and be looking for ways to do business with you at another time. By saying no at the right time, you build a bridge to future business.

5. You just don't have time.

Successful salespeople are always prospecting. They always have possibilities awaiting them. They don't have to make every single sale, because they know there are plenty of other opportunities down the line. If you've been keeping up your cold-calling and prospecting, you will have put together a good client roster. There may be times, however, when you feel that your roster is overflowing, and you just don't have the time and attention a new customer demands. It might be that you cannot handle another account without overextending yourself. If you know that you won't be able to deliver high-quality service to all your customers, it's time to say no. If possible, recommend another vendor. That way, the prospect knows you're looking out for his or her needs, even if you can't take care of them yourself right now. And always make sure the prospect knows that you look forward to working together at some future date.

Successful salespeople learn how to walk away from certain deals. The secret of their success is the massive amount of activity they put into getting qualified customers. If you don't make many calls, you decrease your chances of making sales. Then, when a prospective sale does come along, you feel that you have to grab for it, regardless of the circumstances. However, the more people you call upon, the more contacts you make, the easier it is to walk away from the ones that might be unprofitable or more of a headache than they're worth.

Nobody ever wants to turn down business. But there are times when saying no makes dollars and sense. And if you say yes to the right people, you'll be spending your most valuable time with your most productive accounts. Be sure you know when a sale is profitable for you and your customer, and when it pays to say no.

CHAPTER RECAP:
NEVER TAKE NO *for an* ANSWER

$$\Bigg[\,\textit{To salespeople, the word } \text{no} \textit{ is more of}\atop\textit{a postponement than a refusal.}\,\Bigg]$$

Getting past the gatekeeper.
- Form relationships with gatekeepers because they often have:
  - Inside information.
  - Hidden power and authority.
  - Ability to spread the word about you and your product.
- Use praise and recognition. Send thank-you notes to acknowledge their help.

Getting through to the decision-maker.
- Send a positive message through voice mail.
- Never take no from a person who can't say yes.
- When the straightforward route fails, try something outrageous.

Be persistent, not pushy.
- Be assertive, not aggressive.
- Keep track of how many messages you've left.
- Go directly to the person you want to speak to— and persist.

You've got the appointment—don't give up.

- Now is the time to turn a prospect into a customer.
- Be sure your prospect understands exactly how your product or service will benefit his company.
- Make sure your prospect has enough information to say yes.

Hang in over the long haul.

- Don't let a long sales cycle discourage you.

Handling objections.

- Objections create opportunities for you to understand the prospect and to find ways your product or service will meet the prospect's needs.
- Your goal is to present your real value to the customers. What makes your product or service unique?
- Use the "feel-felt-found" method.
  1. I understand how you feel.
  2. Many of my customers felt the same way.
  3. But when they found . . .

When "Never take no . . ." doesn't apply.

- Five reasons for saying no to a sale:
  1. The sale goes against your goals and priorities.
  2. You can't deliver.
  3. You don't like dealing with the customer.
  4. The customer is better off with another vendor.
  5. You just don't have time.

3 The Relationship Is Everything

Ever since selling began, sales pundits have been trying to come up with a magic formula that would make all sales go like this:

"All great business is based on friendship."

—J. C. PENNEY

walk in the door, say the magic words, ask the one great opening question, handle the one big objection, close the sale.

But every salesperson who lives and works in the real world knows there's no such thing. There are no magic words to get in the door and no easy formula to close the sale. That's why most successful people in this business don't spend their time searching for easy answers. They spend much of their time learning and practicing and honing their sales techniques, but they spend *most* of their time building relationships with their customers.

Not long ago, I was trying to get a large company to buy some of my books to distribute to their franchisees. The client actually had said no twice, but I kept calling with new information and new ways that my product could benefit her company. During one conversation, she happened to mention that her house needed a paint job.

"*I'll* paint your house," I said jokingly. "Buy my books and I'll do the whole job for you."

She started to laugh, and I knew our relationship had changed. That afternoon, I bought a paintbrush and selected some color samples and overnighted them to her with a letter that said, "I'm ready to start painting, and I'll never, ever give up!" About a month later, there was a message from her on my voice mail saying, "Barry—get ready to start painting. We selected your book!" The company ended up buying over twenty thousand copies, and later my client told me she'd framed the paintbrush and samples and has them hanging on her wall.

No sale is made by one factor alone. Sales are made up of all the things you say and do along the way, leading to the close. And, of course, the product has to be right for the prospect. Often, however, the one thing that gets you past barriers and through objections is the relationship you form with the customer.

You never know where sales relationships will lead. Hal Becker, author of *Can I Have Five Minutes of Your Time?* and formerly the number-one sales rep out of eleven thousand reps at Xerox, tells the story of a would-be client he began dealing with in 1977. The prospect needed a copier, but he didn't want to spend the money.

"The first time I met him," says Becker, "I offered to make some free copies for him and he seemed genuinely grateful. He didn't buy anything, but he told me to come back again, so I'd stop in to see him from time to time. He never wanted to buy, but if he needed a hundred copies, I'd go back to my office and make them for him. I knew that when he was ready, he would buy from me."

Fast-forward twelve years. Becker had left Xerox to start his own company and was now looking to sell it to someone he trusted. He told his business broker that although money was important, it was *more* important to find someone with whom a deal could be based more on a handshake than on a contract.

"My broker set up one particular meeting that several people were going to attend," says Becker. "I walked into the conference room and who was the lead investor of the group? My reluctant copier client from 1977. We made a deal right then and there without ever having to look at a contract—all because of the relationship we'd established so many years before when I never even made the sale."

[You Never Get *a* Second Chance *to* Make *a* First Impression]

Since becoming a successful salesperson depends on earning the trust and respect of potential buyers, this is a process that must be practiced continually. Not only are you selling your product; you're also selling yourself.

You begin selling yourself from the moment you decide to call on a potential customer. It starts with your preparation for the call—doing your research about the company, knowing the questions you want to ask, writing down the three key benefits of your product or service, assembling and organizing your sales materials. Only after this kind of thorough preparation are you ready for your first contact.

Here are six keys to help you sell yourself to customers and make a powerful first impression.

1. Begin on a high note.

Emotions are catching. If you walk into a meeting and you let it show that you're in a bad mood, or depressed, or anxious, or exhausted, your prospect will slide right down to your level. On the other hand, if you're upbeat and enthusiastic, your prospect will want to ride that wave right along with you. It's especially important that you be in an upbeat mood the first time you meet someone. A prospect who's having a hard day doesn't want to know that you feel that way, too. He wants to feel that your visit with him is a high spot in your day and that you've been looking forward to meeting him.

There are times when, for whatever reason, you're not really looking forward to meeting a new prospect. You may have to psych yourself up, to pump up the adrenaline and make that call as if it were your best day ever; in other words, "fake it to make it." Instead of concentrating on yourself and how you feel, focus on why you're there: to do something beneficial for the buyer. This becomes easier to do over time as you realize the advantages to yourself, your client, and your sale when you are in this state of mind.

2. The eyes have it.

Twelve years ago, when I was about to go into business for myself, I asked a good friend if he had any advice. His simple words of wisdom? "Make eye contact." There's no substitute for looking a person in the eye, smiling sincerely, and saying, "Hey, it's nice to meet you."

When you're presenting a sales idea, or any time that you're making an important point, be sure to look right into the eyes of the other person. If you're explaining the benefits of your product to a prospect while you're looking down at your papers or over your prospect's shoulder, your words may be telling the prospect one thing, but your eyes will communicate a lack of confidence.

"You have to practice it," says Larry Prince, manager of sales development and planning at Roche Pharmaceuticals.

"You have to tell yourself that even though this person might be intimidating or that person has a reputation for being terse with salespeople, you'll still look them in the eye."

3. A firm grip.

Many a good impression has been undermined by an ineffectual handshake or one that is overly vigorous. Handshakes are second only to eye contact in conveying or betraying self-confidence. Stuart Cohen, vice president of vacation.com, a company that promotes Caribbean cruises, is emphatic: "Handshakes rule! The physical contact of the two hands meeting gives you an unparalleled degree of bonding. But you've got to do it right; you've got to practice. I extend my arm early as a display of eagerness and friendliness to break the ice. I concentrate on allowing our hands to grasp fully and firmly, and I adjust my grip to the other person's, making sure it is equally firm. Simultaneously, my eyes remain laser-fixed on their eyes, and I smile and say their name—twice if it's our first meeting."

4. Have your questions ready.

Stuart Cohen also believes that the way to get those potentially awkward first few moments flowing is to go in prepared with several opening questions: "These are simple, general questions used to engage a prospect. Asking questions promotes conversation and immediately creates a more relaxed environment. The only statements I make up front are to introduce myself and to express gratitude for sharing this time with me."

When Cohen meets a prospect who doesn't know him or his company, he tries to get the person talking while he spends his time listening. "I ask them questions like 'What have you heard about me or my company?' 'What are your perceptions? What do you think is good about my company and what do you think is bad?' That way, I get to hear all the objections at the outset. I take notes while they're speaking, then I gently fill in the blanks, supporting the correct perceptions and correcting the wrong ones."

Another approach is to start with a few brief statements that let prospects know who you are and then get them talking about themselves. If you've worked with companies or industries related to theirs, you might say, "I've worked with Acme Widgets and Ace Machines for many years, helping them to decrease their production time. But before we talk about my company, I'd like to find out more about you and your organization. I want to find out if there's a fit between our two companies, and if there's some value I can bring to your organization like I brought to the others." You can then proceed to ask them questions that help you determine their needs and wants, and how your company, product, or service can fill those needs.

5. To serve, not to sell.

Whenever you go in to see a client, but especially when you meet someone for the first time, you have to go in wearing your problem-solving hat. Your objective is to help this prospect find solutions, to increase his business and his profits.

If you're going in with the purpose of pushing your product, you're going to have to work very, very hard to make that sale. On the other hand, a sale becomes a natural progression when you go in with a focus on how you can meet the needs and desires of and bring value to this individual and his company. That may mean using some creative thinking along with your knowledge and experience to come up with ways to improve your customer's bottom line. This is the time to ask yourself, "What can I do differently? What would be the ideal solution to this problem, and how close can I come to making that happen?"

You might not have solutions at the tip of your fingers at the first meeting, but the prospect needs to know that you've got his problems and concerns firmly in your mind, and that you can come back with ways you (and your product or service) might be able to help.

6. Lighten up.

Over the years, the sales profession has earned itself a shady reputation. Although most salespeople are honest and hard-working, customers are understandably guarded when dealing with people they don't know. One of the best ways to break through a customer's wall of caution is with humor.

I learned this years ago when I started cold-calling door-to-door. Often there was a sign on the door that said, NO SOLICITING, and I would walk in and tell the receptionist, "Hi. I'm with No Soliciting, Incorporated. I wonder if I could speak to the person in charge of buying signs." Once I got the receptionist to smile, I could go on to say, "I wonder if you could help me out. . . ." Most of the time, the answer would be yes.

If I'd gone in instantly pitching myself and my product, I probably would have been shown the door instead of a friendly face. I once read a saying on the bottom of a shampoo bottle, of all places (you never know where you'll run into a good cliché), that said, "Those who blow their own horn never play a good tune." If you're meeting someone for the first time and you talk about yourself the whole time, what impression are you making?

We usually think that to make a good impression we've got to immediately let people know how good we are. But a good impression is more often made by making them feel comfortable, recognized, and important. Let them know you're serious about your profession, but that you don't take yourself too seriously.

[Second Chances]

Of course, nothing can beat starting off on the right foot with a good impression and maintaining it over time. But not every call turns out the way you hoped it would. Every salesperson has walked out of a meeting saying, "That was the worst call I ever made." First of all, you have to figure out if it really didn't go well or if it was really FEAR: False Evidence Appearing Real. The customer may not view the meeting the way you did.

Ann Hanford is a member of Chairman's Circle of Val-Pak, which means she has one of the highest sales percentages in her company (there are only twenty-two members out of twelve hundred sales reps). She agrees that we can't always depend on our own judgment to tell us how we did. "Everybody has an off day once in a while," she says. "But the funny thing is that usually when you think you had an off day, you were really just fine. When I least expect to hear back from somebody, they'll call me and tell me how excited they are about getting started with Val-Pak. Or if I don't hear from them, I'll just call them back and say, 'I felt I was a little off the other day when I saw you. Do you have any questions I can answer for you today?'"

Most people are willing to forgive the human mistakes we make. In fact, they'd rather deal with someone who has slight imperfections than with someone who comes to them with a prepared, memorized sales pitch. People want to buy from human beings, not from robots or fact sheets. I once wanted to send a gift to a customer at Federal Express to thank him for his business. It was a nice gesture on my part—except that I sent it to him by UPS. It was a careless error, but the client thought it was funny and kids me about it to this day.

There may be times when you inherit a bad impression. You may call on a prospect who had a negative experience with your company in the past. Is there any way to get such prospects to take another look at what you have to offer? Stuart Cohen of vacation.com thinks there is. "I ask them to explain the challenges (not problems) they encountered with my company, or things they may have heard. I listen intently, taking notes the whole time. I don't interrupt. I acknowledge what those challenges were by repeating them. I try to convey that I'm taking this situation even more seriously than they are. Then I go on to correct their misperceptions or tell them how the company has changed."

One way you can prove to a wary prospect that you know how to deal with challenges is to get testimonials from customers who are pleased with your service or product, especially from some who had problems with your company that were satisfactorily solved. It's one thing for you to tell prospects how you handle things that go wrong; it's another for them to hear it as a third-party endorsement.

[
People Don't Care How Much You Know Until They Know How Much You Care
]

A few years ago, Robert Shipley, vice president of customer management for Unilever Home and Personal Care (a division of Helene Curtis), was looking for a top rep for the company's health and beauty division. Like most large corporations, Helene Curtis is divided into product categories, and sales reps often spend their entire career in one division. One salesperson in particular had been the number-one sales rep in the coffee division for twenty years. Shipley wanted to move him into his division.

He expected that the rep would feel some anxiety about moving out of his familiar product line and into health and beauty. After all, the products and channels of distribution were totally different. But this sales rep didn't seem to mind the change at all.

"Within six months he was our number-one rep," says Shipley. "He understood that his strength lay in building relationships with people, in understanding and fulfilling their needs.

"What it comes down to," says Shipley, "is that it isn't the product that makes the salesperson, it's understanding what the product can do for the customer."

Which brings us to one of the most important qualities a salesperson can possess—empathy, the ability to understand and appreciate what's most important to another human being. Customers look for salespeople who demonstrate this quality, who are sincerely interested in them and in their business.

What is the impression you make when you demonstrate this interest? The impression is that you care.

A famous study conducted by the Rockefeller Institute several years ago revealed six major reasons customers stopped buying. Sixty-eight percent of defectors left because of an "attitude of indifference shown by one or more representatives of the supplier." Those customers felt that the salesperson just didn't care enough. Only 14 percent left because they were dissatisfied with the product. Another 9 percent left for competitive reasons, and the remainder cited reasons such as prior connections. So the vast majority of those people surveyed stopped buying because of a negative impression brought on by the salesperson's attitude of indifference.

One way to avoid giving an impression of indifference is to show your customers you know what they're about. What challenges are they facing? How can you help them? What motivates this company or this individual? How can you tap into what's most important to that company or individual?

When customers see a salesperson doing something beyond what is expected, it creates a high level of trust. John Dowling, known as "Mr. Commercial Real Estate," believes that extensive research is the key that enables you to go that extra mile. In one instance, Dowling had negotiated a generous electricity allowance for one of his clients. The credit was to be applied to overtime air-conditioning charges. When the bills came in, however, electricity usage was much higher than he had projected and the credit wasn't there. Dowling wanted to know why, so he flew to New Orleans to check the client's meters.

"My hotel room faced their building," says Dowling, "so I sat in my room and photographed their offices during the night. We found out that on all five floors of his offices, the lights stayed on all night."

The client began turning the lights off, but Dowling was still not satisfied. He sent in a team to investigate, and eventually motion detectors were installed. These devices saved the client hundreds of thousands of dollars because the lights go off automatically when people leave the rooms.

It's not necessary to get on a plane or stay up all night to show you care. Many salespeople use profile sheets to help them keep track and remember the things they learn about a customer—things like birthdays, marital status and children, special interests, goals and objectives, and so on. Then, the next time they speak to the person, they can make a comment about something they spoke about previously. For instance, if the prospect happened to mention that his daughter played soccer, you can ask how well her team did in the league. Or if a prospect says that she prizes punctuality above all other virtues, you'll know that you must never be late for a meeting with her.

[Developing Friendly Relationships]

If we could become friends with all our customers, the selling life would be much simpler. It's not only customers who want to do business with people they like, trust, and respect; salespeople want that, too. And some customers may become real friends, people with whom you have a personal as well as business relationship. But for the most part, the best we can do is build relationships that are as congenial as possible.

"You have to treat your customers the way you want to be treated," says Richard Green, a top sales rep with Marriott's National Account Group, who is so good at building relationships that his customers throw parties for him instead of vice versa. "We all have these distinctions between buyers, sellers, customers . . . there really isn't a difference. We're all just people. People really do buy from people they like and trust, and if you can make a client like you, you have a much better chance of getting the business."

> *"Genius is the capacity for seeing relationships where lesser men see none."*
>
> —WILLIAM JAMES

Green enjoys entertaining, so he often brings clients to his home and cooks dinner for them. "Entertaining at home brings things to a totally different level," he says. "Clients love knowing how you live away from the office. They love getting to know the essence of a person. And what better way than seeing a person's home?"

Of course, you're not going to invite all your clients to your home. But there are moments when sharing a meal is appropriate and useful for strengthening the relationship. In many cultures, there's a tradition of making deals while breaking bread that creates a stronger bond than any contract.

It's amazing how little effort it actually takes to form a friendly relationship. Michael Leiss, vice president of consumer sales for Gateway Computers, tells about a time when his company's customer satisfaction ratings had declined. The company did some research, surveying people who called Gateway, got information, and then didn't buy. They found that the number-one reason people turned to a competitor was that they didn't feel the Gateway sales rep was friendly! So Gateway began to train its reps to be friendly and enthusiastic, even down to the simple, almost clichéd practice of smiling when they spoke to people on the phone. Since the program was instituted, Gateway has seen a 15 to 20 percent increase in closing sales.

Customers don't expect to become bosom buddies with you. They do want to know that you value them as human beings (not just as a means of income) and that you're sincerely interested in helping them reach their goals. Everyone in life, after all, wants to find someone who's sincere and will help them make their life easier.

[It's *a* Matter *of* Trust]

Your customers rely on your honesty, your integrity, your ability to deliver on your word. They don't have time to research every detail about your products; they rely on you to do it for them.

It's easy to build trust with people who are your customers now. It's more difficult—and often more essential—to build trust and relationships *before* someone is your customer. Unless you're dealing with a brand-new company, most people already have a supplier of whatever it is you're selling. You have to give them a reason to break up an established relationship in favor of your product or service.

When Bill Carigan was regional sales manager for Hollander Manufacturing, makers of modular structural fittings, he was struggling to get business from a manufacturer of playground equipment. The manufacturer felt he could get a similar fitting for a lower price, and was not willing to switch. But Carigan wouldn't give up.

He kept calling on the manufacturer with new ideas. He went to the installation sites and asked the installers about how he could help make the installations easier. Then he presented the prospect with designs based on their own installers' feedback. "We were establishing our commitment to be a partner with them, even before we had their business," says Carigan.

Then, late one Saturday afternoon, Carigan received a call from the potential customer. They were installing a playground in South Bend, Indiana, and were short one fitting. The had called their regular supplier, but had no luck. The prospect said, "You're always talking about service. We're supposed to have a grand opening on Monday, and without that fitting, we won't make it. What can you do to help us out?"

It was too late for Carigan's distributors on the East Coast to be open, so he called one in California, who was not only open, but had the right fitting in stock. A shipment arrived at the playground on Sunday, and the opening went off without a hitch.

"If I hadn't found that distributor in California," says Carigan, "we would have opened our foundry, made a fitting, and driven the part to South Bend. This was the start of a long-term relationship that has brought in millions of dollars to

Hollander. It was the fact that we were committed to this relationship before we had the account that won us the business. Sometimes, you have to prove that you can be a better partner for your customer than their current supplier."

There are times when it takes years to build the kind of relationship that results in a large sale. In 1996, Dean Richards was working for Océ copiers and was hoping to make the Los Angeles County Department of Social Services a client. At the time, they were using more than twelve hundred copiers throughout the county.

"It took us two and a half years to build relationships with the county's Board of Supervisors because we were a company they'd never heard of before," says Richards. "They had to learn to trust the Océ sales team.

"We tried to figure out what was most important to them and help them meet their goals. The Department of Social Services held an annual golf tournament for charity. We donated fifteen thousand dollars as a sponsor. We provided T-shirts for a walk-a-thon. We got involved with community affairs so they'd know we weren't just trying to sell them a product but also wanted to be genuine partners who were going to be around for the long haul."

Those trust-building efforts really paid off. The result—$12 million of hardware revenue—was the largest sale in the history of Océ. "The county trusted us because they believed that we were interested in what mattered to them," says Richards. This trust was not built between Océ and the Department of Social Services. It was built between the individuals involved in the sale.

CHAPTER RECAP:
THE RELATIONSHIP IS EVERYTHING

[
*Often, the one thing that gets you past barriers
and through objections is the relationship
that you form with your customer.*
]

The six keys to making a powerful first impression are:

1. Begin on a high note.
2. Make eye contact.
3. Practice a firm handshake.
4. Have your questions ready.
5. Remember you're there to serve, not to sell.
6. Lighten up.

You can have a second chance.

- Evaluate your meeting: Did it really not go well or was it FEAR—False Evidence Appearing Real?
- Deal with inherited negative impressions by correcting misperceptions or letting the customer know how things have changed.
- Use testimonials from satisfied customers.
- Never make the same mistake twice.

People don't care how much you know until they know how much you care.
- It isn't the product that makes the salesperson; it's understanding what your customers want and what you can do for them.
- One of the most important qualities you can possess is empathy—the ability to understand and appreciate what is most important to another human being.
- Learn as much as you can about your prospects, and take notes to remember what you've learned.

Develop friendly relationships.
- Treat your customers the way you want to be treated.
- Let customers know you value them as human beings, not just as a means of income.

It's a matter of trust.
- Your customers rely on your honesty, integrity, and ability to deliver on your word. They can't always try your product before they buy, so they have to believe what you tell them.
- Trust is not built between companies. It is built between individuals involved in the sale.

4 Your ATTITUDE Determines Your Altitude

I f an extraterrestrial had managed to land on planet Earth in the 1980s, it would have come to the conclusion that the only thing humans ever talked about was attitude. Attitude was everywhere. Positive this, positive that. Change your attitude and you'll change your life. Bookshelves were packed with attitude; television talk shows and infomercials featured a myriad of inspirational gurus; and car stereo systems played motivational recordings up and down America's highways. Corporations paid hundreds of thousands of dollars for inspirational speakers.

Come the nineties, everyone was saying, "Enough already. What else can you talk about?" Attitude was passé; Pollyanna was past her prime. We all started looking for new ideas and different topics. And that was understandable . . . but unfortunate.

Because, cliché or no, attitude is still and will always be one of the most important factors in anyone's success in business (or in life for that matter). It's what enables some people to move forward and what holds others back.

[The Great Equalizer]

Picture yourself waking up in the morning and thinking about the day ahead. The day holds the possibilities of great financial rewards and personal satisfaction, but you know the odds: every phone call you make, every meeting you attend, and every letter you write invites rejection. You'll make dozens of calls asking people to buy what you sell, and more often than not the answer will be no. In fact, whole days may go by without a single yes. Week in and week out you have to face the likelihood of rejection, obstacles, failures, and setbacks.

Salespeople are made of the same stuff as every other human being. If you didn't get discouraged and depressed sometimes, you'd be a robot. It's part of the life you've chosen, the living you make. But the most successful salespeople are those who can maintain a positive attitude despite the rejections. It's not that they go around whistling a happy tune all day. It's that they don't let the rough times shape their world.

Harvey Mackay, author of *Swim with the Sharks Without Being Eaten Alive,* is also chairman and CEO of Mackay Envelope Corporation, a company that has been in business since the 1950s. He believes that attitude is the cornerstone of living. "I've studied attitude for over forty years now," he says. "I have a ten-step process for hiring, but number one on my list is attitude. You get your choice when you get up every morning. Every single morning, you can be either an optimist or a pessimist. You can be happy, you can be sad, you can have the right attitude, or you can have the wrong attitude. When I look to hire someone, I'm looking for someone who makes a good choice every morning, someone who's got a phenomenal attitude and the 'stick-to-it' mentality to hang in through rough times."

When we talk about attitude and sales, we're talking about the way you take on a day. Do you think about the possibilities that lie ahead or past and future disasters? George Bernard Shaw said, "The people who get on in this world are the people who get up and look for the circumstances

> *"Attitude . . . fuels my fire or assaults my hope. When my attitude's aright, there's no barrier too high, no valley too deep, no dream too extreme, no challenge too great for me."*
>
> —CHARLES SWINDOLL

they want, and if they cannot find them, make them." It's easy to blame setbacks and failures on "circumstances." There are many things that happen beyond our control. We get into trouble when we let those circumstances control what happens next.

Liesa Wiele is a senior account manager for Wire One Technologies, a Virginia-based company that sells video conferencing equipment. She is one of their top five sales performers. "All salespeople have had experiences where they've worked really hard—and lost the deal anyway," says Wiele. "There was one instance where I spent several months building relationships and negotiating with a particular company to sell them conferencing equipment. What I didn't know was that they had already decided on another vendor, but were talking to me because company policy required that they had to get competitive bids. I really thought I was going to make this sale, and I was very disappointed when it didn't go through.

"But my attitude is this: When a deal falls through, you keep your composure, congratulate the prospects on their decision, and let them know that the door is always open if there is ever anything you can do for them. I told myself, 'Just because I didn't get the hardware deal doesn't mean I can't go back to them in a little while and propose something else they might need.' I didn't waste the time I spent with them—I got to know the people in that company and what their needs were, so that I was able to go back to them later on and make a different sale."

If you're out there, pushing yourself past the norms in your industry, you're going to encounter both obstacles and rejection. Your attitude has to be strong enough to withstand all the hits it's going to take. The best salespeople take each new day as a challenge. They're never complacent, for they never know what a day might bring.

[The Importance *of* Enthusiasm]

Enthusiasm is the frosting on the attitude cake. If you're a salesperson, you know that although you sell a product or service, what a customer buys is *you*. A positive attitude lets you deal with whatever happens to you in life, and enthusiasm lets you do it with excitement and energy.

Enthusiasm comes from the Greek word *entheos,* which means "inspired" or "having god within." It's almost like an electrical current that creates attraction. People like to be around genuine enthusiasm. Your enthusiasm invites people to join you in your belief about what you're selling. It shows in your voice, in your body language, in your willingness to do whatever you can to provide your customers with the best possible service.

Burt Stanier, chairman of Knoll, Inc. (a global manufacturer of office furnishings), specifically looks for enthusiasm when he hires new salespeople. "At Knoll, we have a sales force of over three hundred people, and it is one of our greatest strengths. A significant portion of their compensation is com- mission- and incentive-based. So we're not looking for followers— we're looking for people who 'want to drive the bus.' They're entrepreneurial. They're result- oriented. They're very deter- mined, and they're enthusiastic. They have to be to succeed.

> *"Flaming enthusiasm, backed by horse sense and persistence, is the quality that most frequently makes for success."*
>
> —DALE CARNEGIE

"This process is very demo- cratic. If you're good at your job, it shows. If you're not, it also shows. It's difficult to say exactly what mix of abilities and personality goes together to make someone successful, but enthusiasm is a major component. To be successful here, you have to be someone who likes the chal- lenge, someone who has a strong, enthusiastic will to win."

[The Power *of* Passion]

If attitude is mind, and enthusiasm is body, then passion is spirit. It's about having a deep love and respect for what you do personally and professionally.

Why does anyone choose to go into a profession where rejection is an everyday occurrence? There is, of course, the possibility of making a lot of money. That may be why people go into sales, but it's not what makes people stay—and stay successful. The most successful salespeople love to sell, and they truly believe in the product or service they're selling. As a result, they communicate that belief and passion to their customers.

Customers are smart enough to see through a false commitment. When you have a genuine passion, you want to know as much as you can about your product, your market, your competition. The most successful salespeople I know—the most successful *people* I know, for that matter—believe in the principle of continuous improvement. They never think they know everything there is to know about their profession. They read everything. They participate in training. They have mentors (and are mentors themselves).

Not only do they know their own business, they know their customers' businesses as well. There's a saying in martial arts: "If you don't know yourself and you don't know your opponent, you'll lose 100 percent of the time. If you know yourself but don't know your opponent, you'll win 50 percent of the time. If you know yourself and know your opponent, you'll win 100 percent of the time." Similarly, in selling, it's important to know your customers—what they need and what you can do to fill those needs. Because, ultimately, you want your customers to be better off as a result of the purchase of your product or service.

"I have a wonderful opportunity every day," says Alan Boyko, vice president of sales for Scholastic Book Fairs, a division of Scholastic, Inc., which publishes the incredibly popular Harry Potter series of books. (The Harry Potter books are among the few children's series to ever hit the adult best-seller list.) Speaking with Boyko is inspirational because of the love he feels for his job. You can see it in his eyes and hear it in his voice:

"I love my product. We make a huge difference. We're educating children. It's a mission I believe in, and one I preach to all our salespeople. We're giving children a better opportunity with every book we sell. A lot of people don't get that kind of satisfaction. If that's the case, they should find something else to do. I think you can be passionate about whatever you sell, whether it's medical supplies, computers, or pencils.

"I was talking to someone this morning who sells brushes. All kinds of brushes. He was very passionate about them and told me all about their many uses, including those in the military and in medical research. It's amazing how passionate he could be about a brush. And how much he loves what he does. That is a successful salesperson.

"He's passionate about brushes; I'm passionate about books. When I was young and I started my own business, I would go to schools with my books. I'd see the faces of all the kids, and I knew they needed these books. People couldn't say no to me. It's a very powerful motivator to know that the more books kids read, the better they get. It wasn't up to them to say no. I wouldn't let them."

Anyone can have this kind of passion. It comes from a belief in yourself, in your abilities, and in your product or service, and it will carry you through all the rejections in the world.

[Persistence *and* Tenacity]

Not all successful salespeople have special skills or talents. What makes them successful is a fierce determination that gets them past obstacles and barriers. It takes persistence to go after a prospective customer who is difficult to reach, who can't make up his mind, or who seems on the verge of buying, only to back out at the last minute. And they have the tenacity to keep making calls every single day in the face of constant resistance and rejection. These are the realities of selling.

The story of John Quinn, manager of radio station WJBM in New Jersey, is a case in point. Several years ago, when an Ikea store opened in Elizabeth, Quinn was determined to get its general manager, Peter Connolly, to advertise on his station. Ikea was concentrating its advertising in national media, but Quinn continued to try to set up a meeting with Connolly. He called him several times and dropped by the store frequently. And although he couldn't get Connolly to talk with him, over time he managed to become friends with Connolly's assistant. He told her he was planning a surprise for her boss and needed to know the route he took to work.

As Connolly relates the story, "I was driving to work on the turnpike one morning when I passed a billboard I'd passed every day for weeks. That morning, the billboard read, 'Peter. Congratulations on your successful store opening. Turn to 1530 AM on your radio. I want to talk to you.'

"I wanted to be sure the message was for me, so I turned on the radio. Sure enough, right away I heard an announcement that said, 'Peter Connolly, we've been trying to get through to you. Can't we please come in and meet with you?' Turns out Quinn had been playing that announcement every five minutes during the time he knew I usually drove to work. Naturally, I couldn't turn down a meeting with him after that. Somebody with that kind of determination was someone I wanted to do business with."

Of course, most salespeople don't have access to a billboard on a major highway—Quinn did because a friend of his owned it—but every salesperson can have the kind of persistence and tenacity that Quinn exhibited. Many salespeople would have given up after being turned down several times, but Quinn, like other successful salespeople, would not give up until he had tried every possible means of reaching his goal.

Quinn's persistence, tenacity, and determination got him the meeting with Connolly. But he made the sale, and kept Ikea as an advertiser, because of the relationship that developed between himself and Connolly. He was honest about what he could do for Ikea and lived up to all promises he made. He even came through on a promise to introduce Connolly to

James Florio, who was then governor of New Jersey. "I don't expect that every salesperson I work with is going to be able to introduce me to the governor," says Connolly. "But I do expect that if you say you're going to do it, you keep your word."

[**Maintaining** *a* **Positive Attitude**]

Unfortunately, we're not all born with a positive attitude. For most of us, it's something that has to be learned and practiced.

Fortunately, there are many ways to build and maintain a positive attitude in the face of adversity:

❏ **Read something inspiring every day.** When you get up in the morning, before you do anything else, spend fifteen minutes reading something motivational, something enlightening. Do the same thing at night for fifteen minutes before you go to bed.

❏ **Find a quote that really means something to you,** cut it out or copy it, and hang it on a wall where you can see it every day. A short quote can take you a million miles. People are always telling me, "I know this might sound silly, but I hang the word *attitude* on my mirror so it's the first thing I see every day." Or "I know it might be corny, but I have a quote I keep in my wallet that I can pull out when I'm having a bad day." These things *might* sound corny, but they work! Sometimes we just need small reminders.

❏ **Take an honest look at the people around you.** What kinds of attitudes do they bring to the table? Do they pump you up or bring you down? Everyone is entitled to a bad attitude now and again—but if the people you know are constantly angry, bitter, or scared, it might be time to find yourself a new crowd.

❏ **Count your blessings,** and think about others who have turned bad attitudes around. I love to watch inspiring movies about people who didn't give up even though they had to fight against heavy odds. Those people claimed their right to own a positive attitude no matter what the circumstance, and in the end were able to reap their rewards.

❏ **Be selective about the books and magazines you read,** the shows and movies you watch, the tapes you listen to. We live in a world of high content; information comes at us from every possible medium. Remember, though, that just as inspiring movies can improve your attitude, too much negative content can have the opposite impact. Nothing determines your attitude—for good or bad—more than the environment with which you choose to surround yourself.

❏ **Find attitude mentors**—people you can call for an infusion of excitement and enthusiasm.

It's easy to let any good habit slide, and sometimes we need reminders to keep ourselves on track. Not long ago, a man called me and told me this story. He had been very depressed, because his company was merging with a larger company and five hundred people were going to be fired. Then he got a memo from his boss about how important it was to maintain a good attitude when things were not going well and that, even though the future looked uncertain, belief in oneself must not waiver. He read the memo, went into his boss's office, and said, "Thanks for this reminder. This is the best memo I ever read. I'm totally pumped up now."

"Well," she said, "I'm glad to hear that. You wrote this memo three years ago."

It's easy to forget the commitments we made when we started out, the fresh attitude we brought to a new career or new environment. It tends to slowly erode with each new rejection. But remembering helps to put job and career in their proper perspective. You can't wait for other people to help you lift your attitude. You can use other people with positive attitudes as examples, but they can't do it for you. Remember that old cliché: If it's to be, it's up to me.

[Attitude *and* Risk]

If you have a strong belief in yourself and your abilities, you'll be more willing to take risks. And you can never be a truly successful salesperson without taking a risk every now and then.

Remember this: There's safety in risk and risk in safety. Risk in itself doesn't mean you take chances blindly without considering the consequences. You take calculated risks, where the chances of success are high. The only way to grow is to push yourself beyond your present limits. Push yourself into areas that are unknown to you. Start selling to new accounts. Find new applications for your product or service. Introduce your product or service to new markets. Try something you've never tried before.

You have to push yourself out there, and that means changing with the competition—changing with the new technologies, changing with consumers' needs Change *is* risk, but there's no other way to move forward. When you take a risk, you've already succeeded—even if you don't reach the goal you set for yourself. Because you grow from it and you come away with a better understanding of what you need to do next time.

Taking a risk also gives you insight into your own character. It lets you see what you're capable of doing. When you see that you're able to get through setbacks and to move past failures, when you see how much you really are able to accomplish, you lay the strongest possible foundation for a positive attitude.

If you're looking for the road to success, you won't find any clear signposts. There's no fairy godmother to grant your wishes for fame and fortune. Of all the successful salespeople and high achievers I work with, not one has taken the same path as any other.

However, what they all have is an attitude of expectation. They expect things to turn out well and have confidence in their own abilities to make that happen. What happens when you ask people if they're going to accomplish their goals? The answer you usually hear is "I'll give it my best shot." But people who believe in themselves, people who have achieved success against the odds, will answer with three of the most powerful words in the English language: "Yes, I will."

They are so positive, and their expectations are so strong, they will prevail over any obstacles in their way. Other people recognize their strength and either move out of the way to let them through or find a way to hop on board.

There are many times in life when we have to risk being wrong. We take risks with money, with time, with energy. We sacrifice one goal to achieve another. But risks can be calculated so that they pay off more times than not.

> *"Any challenge facing us is not as important as our attitude toward it, for that determines our success or failure."*
>
> —NORMAN VINCENT PEALE

When you lose sight of risk, you lose sight of opportunity. As author Erica Jong once said, "The truth is, if you don't risk anything, you risk even more."

[Give It All You Have]

Just looking into the mirror and telling yourself how wonderful you are, then going out and doing just what you've always done, won't change your life at all. High achievers know you have put in the time and effort necessary to increase your chances of success. You have to research new accounts thoroughly before you approach them. You've got to study many different markets for your products until you find ones that present possibilities. You may face obstacles, but you must be prepared to work through them.

People who hire salespeople say the two most important traits they look for are:

- A very strong attitude.
- A desire to make the effort.

These two traits make a winning combination. A positive attitude stimulates effort, and effort reinforces a positive attitude.

If you study the truly successful people in the sales field, you'll find that none of them sees being in sales as a nine-to-five job. They put in the effort required to achieve their goals.

As Rieva Lesonsky, vice president and editorial director of Entrepreneur Media, says, "You have to put the time in. When you're starting a business, money is probably your smallest investment. You need to invest a lot of time and energy. But if you can't maintain a positive attitude, particularly in light of the fact that mistakes are going to happen, you're going to be in a lot of trouble. I don't think you can achieve without a positive attitude."

Your attitude forms every moment of your day, whether you realize it or not. Your attitude determines your enjoyment of life and your gratitude for all your blessings, but also your disappointment and anger at how things have turned out. It determines your productivity and satisfaction from accomplishments small and large, but also the feeling that no accomplishment will ever be good enough.

There are some circumstances in life we can change; there are many we cannot. When we are faced with situations we must accept, we have two options: we can live in disappointment, bitterness, and anger, or we can look within ourselves, find that place that won't be crushed by circumstance, and then . . . pick ourselves up, dust ourselves off, and start all over again.

CHAPTER RECAP:
YOUR ATTITUDE DETERMINES YOUR ALTITUDE

[*Attitude is the most important factor in anyone's success in business—and in life.*]

Attitude is the great equalizer.
- Successful salespeople maintain a positive attitude despite rejection.

The importance of enthusiasm.
- It's the frosting on the attitude cake.
- Live up to the meaning of enthusiasm: "the god within."
- Perform your job with energy and excitement.

The power of passion.
- Have a strong belief in the product or service you're selling.
- Communicate that belief to your customers.
- Perfect the art of continuous improvement—read, participate in training, cultivate mentors.
- Know your own business and your customers' businesses as well.

Persistence and tenacity.
- Continue to pursue your objectives despite obstacles.
- Do not become easily discouraged.
- Try many different means of reaching your goals.

Maintain a positive attitude.

- Read something inspiring every day.
- Find a quote that means something to you and hang it where you can see it every day.
- If the people around you are constantly angry, bitter, or scared, find yourself a new crowd.
- Be selective about the books and magazines you read, the shows and movies you watch, and the tapes you listen to.
- Find attitude mentors you can call for an infusion of excitement and enthusiasm.

Attitude and risk.

- If you believe in yourself and your abilities, you'll be more willing to take risks.
- There's risk in safety and safety in risk.
- Change is risk, but there's no other way to move forward.
- Expect things to turn out well and have confidence in your own abilities to make them happen.

Give it all you have.

- To be a high achiever, you have to put in the time and effort necessary to lessen the possibility of failure.
- A positive attitude stimulates effort, and effort reinforces a positive attitude.
- It's not what you look at that counts, but how you look at it.
- When you are faced with less-than-perfect situations, you have two choices: you can live in disappointment or you can pick yourself up, dust yourself off, and start all over again.

5 The HARDER You Work, *the* LUCKIER You Get

Some people think you have to be lucky to be successful. You have to be born talented or rich or well connected, or you have to be in the right place at the right time. In fact, some people use other people's "luck" as a defense against success. They say, "I could be successful, too, if I had what he had!"

The fact is that those people will never be successful, no matter what they're handed or how it comes to them. They

"The dictionary is the only place where success comes before work."

—ARTHUR BRISBANE

don't understand that luck is a reward for the hard work you've put in to reach your goal. You don't just run into luck. You earn it.

Of course, things do happen by chance every once in a while. You might be at your daughter's Little League game and run into someone whose company has been looking for a product just like yours. You might make a cold call to a large account that others have been working on for months, happen to catch someone in immediate need of your service, and make a sale. But your "lucky break" will take you only so far. You've got to be able to put in the effort and follow through.

Luck is created by increasing the frequency of those activities that are most likely to lead to success. For instance, a salesperson who calls on ten people will be luckier in terms of finding a viable prospect than will a salesperson who calls on two people. There's no getting around it: it takes effort to get lucky. Tiny pieces of luck seep into every small step you take toward your goal. Put all those steps together, and you've got that lucky break!

Or, as the writer and educator Shelby Steele once said, "Opportunity follows struggle. It follows effort. It follows hard work. It doesn't come before."

I speak to some of the highest achievers in the country in business, sports, and entertainment, and they all tell me the same thing: the one trait that has made them more successful than most other people is working past the general work ethic, putting more work into their job than the next person.

It's that extra push that makes the difference, whether it's finding ways to get new prospects, serving current customers, or working with a vendor. What counts most is the "behind-the-scenes" effort that your prospects and customers don't witness.

Hard work is never glamorous. Nobody sees it. There are no television shows that begin with the announcer saying, "Today we're interviewing the successful salesperson Bob Jones of Acme Corporation. Ladies and gentlemen, this is incredible. It's nine P.M. He's put his kids to bed and now he's sitting at his desk, planning his schedule for next week, putting together packets of material and writing thank-you notes. What a champ."

So what causes high achievers to put in the extra effort? Sure, they have pressures and obligations like everyone else, bills they have to pay and goals they want to meet. But that's not why they do it. They do it because they like to do it and they want to enjoy the benefits that hard work brings, a few of which follow.

1. It makes you feel good.
Simple, but true. When you don't work hard, you can get drawn into the path of complacency that leads toward procrastination and then into desperation because of the things you have not yet accomplished. Work, especially hard work, gives us an unequaled sense of accomplishment. Nothing quite matches the satisfaction of a job well done, of attaining the goals you've set out to achieve. And when you know that you have put in the hours and the effort, you can relax and enjoy the leisure time you do have.

2. It affects your attitude.

When your work is more valuable to you, you're more valuable to your work. When you feel good about the work you do, it comes across to customers. When work becomes more than just a fast buck, it's a true expression of how you value your time and energy—and how you value your customers' time and energy as well.

3. It provides added value to customers.

Customers appreciate the hard work you put in for them. In a poll of more than one hundred buyers from the National Association of Purchasing Managers, a strong work ethic was one of the ten most valued attributes of a salesperson. Customers want to know that if they run into a problem, you'll be there to help them out—even if it means working late in the day or over the weekend. They want to know that you'll put in a 110 percent effort to make their business grow (which makes your business grow as well). They see a hardworking rep as someone who honestly cares about them and their business.

4. It's an insurance policy for you and for your customers.

Hard work is the only insurance that your business will move forward. You're investing now for your future, just as you would with an insurance policy. And when your customers see that you're someone who works hard, they trust that you'll take care of their accounts. If customers know that when they buy a product or service from you, you're going to be their advocate and will follow through and make sure that what you promised is delivered, they'll come to trust you. When you have earned their trust, they'll buy from you and keep buying from you, rather than having to learn to trust somebody else.

You are the only one who can make the decision about how hard you're willing to work. There's another old sales cliché (they just keep coming, don't they?) that says, "Sales is the highest-paid hard work and the lowest-paid easy work." When you work really hard at sales and move to the top of your field, it's possible to make a lot of money, sometimes even more than the CEO or president of the company. On the other hand, if you choose to make just a few calls and go home at three in the afternoon, you may not get much in return, but it can be easy work. It's easy to slack off and do just enough to get by; most of the time, nobody's watching you when you're out in the field.

[It's Not How Hard You Work, It's How Smart You Work]

How can I say this when I just finished extolling the rewards and advantages of working hard? Because hard work by itself doesn't always guarantee success. Many people work hard all their lives, but they don't work smart and they don't achieve success. Working smart is the ability to make sure that while you work hard, you use the most productive means possible to get the job accomplished. It's the ability to do a task, evaluate it, and see how that task can be done better the next time. It's discovering how you can become more efficient each time you do something. It's understanding what your strengths are and building on them. It's when you convert every step you take into something that gives you even more benefit the next time you take it.

The best way to work smart is to manage the time you have so that you know what kinds of tasks you have to accomplish and the best times to accomplish them. That often means dividing your time into face-to-face (or voice-to-voice) sales time and nonselling activity time.

In a sales management training seminar I lead, I use an exercise called the "Time Management Test." I designed it for managers to give to their whole team, but there's no reason it can't apply to individual salespeople. It's really very simple. Here's how it goes: Starting on Monday, keep a journal of what you're doing every hour that you're working. If you start at 9:00, stop work at 9:55 and record what your last hour's activity has been. Do the same thing at the end of each hour throughout the day. On Friday, compare that week's activity and productivity to the week before. I guarantee you will have accomplished more during your journal-keeping week.

Why? Because you had to think about everything you did. You were forced to think about the hour you just spent and how you could have improved it, and the hour to come and how you're going to spend it. It's proactive thinking about how you can work more efficiently, whether that means increasing your time in front of customers or on the phone, changing the time of day during which you do paperwork, or changing your driving route so that you spend less time on the road. You automatically start allocating your time more wisely.

This test is all about the ability to look at the big picture and take the time to think about what you can do to work smarter. Sometimes, that's all it takes—not making giant changes, but taking the time to think about what you're doing and what small changes you can make to improve your overall efficiency.

Another important aspect of working smart is knowing how and when you work best. This will be different for everyone. Learn to tap into your own body rhythms. If you work best in the mornings, try to schedule your most important activities during the first hours of the day. If afternoon is best, that's when you need to be doing peak-energy activities. The only way to make these discoveries is through trial and error.

Some people work hard at a steady pace throughout the day or week. Other people work hard in spurts. That's the category I fit into. There are times (when I know I don't have client commitments) that I take half a day off to be with my family. But then, when I go back to work, I'll go at it for five or six hours straight, and I can accomplish more in that time than if I had worked through the whole day.

You're the only one who can determine what works best for you. You experiment, you fail, you try again, you fail again, and then you get it. The cold, hard fact is that it takes time and effort to learn the best ways to spend your time and effort.

We all have our own ways of making work more effective, but no one I know has a magic wand that makes it easy. And I don't know anyone who is highly successful who doesn't work hard. The reason most books and tapes don't stress this fact is that it's not what most people want to hear; it's not new or fresh or exciting. It's as old as work itself, and even with all our great new technology, working hard is still the best way up the ladder.

[Speaking *of the* New Technology . . .]

Where does technology fit into the mix of working smart? Does every salesperson need technology to succeed? And how does technology affect the all-important relationships salespeople rely on for their business?

If anyone knows the answers to those questions, it's George Colombo, founder of Influence Technologies and author of *Capturing Customers.com.* Colombo is an expert on the subject of technology-enabled sales and marketing—how to use technology to make sales more efficient and productive.

For Colombo, there are three main ways that technology helps salespeople work smarter.

1. Automating tasks you don't have time to do.

There are now many software programs that automate tasks for salespeople, such as tracking prospects' information (who you called, when you called them, when to follow up, etc.) and purchasing information (who bought what, when they bought it, when payment was received). Some software can provide an overview of where you are in the sales cycle with various customers, and can generate lists of the top ten (or any number) customers who have spent the highest dollar volume over a particular time period. These kinds of tasks, which used to take several hours, can now be accomplished in seconds.

Many small tasks, such as sending thank-you notes, can now be accomplished with almost no effort. Every salesperson knows how effective it is to send a thank-you note as soon as possible after you've had an initial meeting or phone call with a prospective customer. It's not a big secret. But the percentage of salespeople who actually send such notes is very small. Often, the only reason it doesn't get done is because there simply isn't enough time in the day. You may feel overwhelmed with paperwork. You may decide that priority should be given to getting out and seeing customers. And you may be right. Technology gives you the opportunity to concentrate on your priorities, by giving you the ability to automate these kinds of simple but important tasks. There are currently several effective software programs that allow you to set up a system that, with the click of a mouse, will generate a thank-you note the day after your meeting and remind you to call the prospect again in ten days (or whatever sequence of events you choose). So it takes you ten seconds to send out a note, instead of ten minutes.

Is this kind of form letter an ideal method of communication? Of course not. But for many salespeople, it's the only kind of communication that will actually get sent. And that means that prospects who used to fall through the cracks can now be turned into viable customers.

"In a perfect world, all your notes would be handwritten and totally personalized," says Colombo. "But for most salespeople, the deciding point is not handwritten versus computer-generated. The deciding point is computer-generated versus not getting it done. If sending a computerized letter is the only way your communication will get sent, then I say go for it."

2. Information accessibility.

The world of sales is changing rapidly. It used to be that all interaction took place between the salesperson and the customer. In today's business environment, however, there are many other people in the company who might wind up speaking to the customer, such as a call center operator, a customer service representative, or someone in shipping or operations. It's become necessary, therefore, for everyone to have access to information about your interactions with your customers.

When account information is loaded into a networked computer system, everyone has access to it. A problem that, in the past, could be solved only by the salesperson can now be solved by a customer service representative who has access to a customer's file. Before computerization, customers used to hear excuses like "You'll have to speak to your salesperson about that" or "I can't help you with this; your salesperson never told me about it." Now, customers can get their problems solved or questions answered in a timely fashion, whether or not they can speak to their sales representative. In addition, it frees the salesperson up to do what he or she needs to do—which is to be out there selling.

3. Adding science to art.

Selling will always be a mix of art and science. It's your art that gets you in the door—your attitude, your persistence and tenacity, your ability to establish relationships. Technology won't make the sale for you, but it can make the entire sales process easier and more effective. It can enhance your sales ability by helping you to research prospects before a sale. Web sites usually reveal immense amounts of information about companies, and you can often find additional relevant information via bulletin boards and search engines. In addition, as we've seen, it can help you to stay in touch with your customers after the sale.

There's no getting away from the fact that technology is an increasing part of everyone's business—and that's a good thing. It can increase your ability to communicate with your customers, and can help you collect data that enable you to strategize and set sales goals. Many customers want to know that you (and/or your company) have the technology to provide the service and support they require.

However, sales are based on personal relationships. It's easy to get so involved in the latest technology that you slack off on the number of calls you make. Every week, I hear from managers who say, "My salespeople need to get out there and generate more business." When I investigate the problem, I often find that the reps are spending too many hours each day inputting data into their computers or dealing with the learning curve of some new gadget—when they should be out selling. Technology is important, but nothing can take the place of the human connection.

[Timing Is Everything]

As a salesperson, you always want to be in the right place at the right time. You want to be the person who comes to mind when potential customers need your product. But since there's no way of knowing when the right time will be, you have to be there *all* the time. You keep calling prospects and customers, sending them notes, faxes, e-mails, and letters with new information. And all of these communications must contain something of value; you want to be looked on as someone who can benefit their company, not as a tiresome pest.

Then one day they say, "You know, we really need one of those widgets now," and it's your name that comes to mind. You kept increasing your value with every bit of new information, and now you've earned the right to get the business.

Sometimes, there's no substitute for the give-and-take of a live conversation, but you have to be careful about just when to call. Certain times are better for particular customers than others. You're not a mind reader; if you happen to call at an inconvenient time, you can apologize and ask when would be a better time. But customers need to feel that their time is as important to you as it is to them. The best salespeople accommodate their schedules to their customers'; they make appointments for 6:30 in the morning, if necessary, or 6:30 at night.

Mark Phillips, a highly successful sales and marketing rep for Val-Pak, finds that the best way to know when to contact prospects and customers is to ask them, "When do you *not* want to be contacted?" That allows him greater flexibility. For example, if a customer says, "Don't call me during lunch hour," that still leaves seven out of eight hours in the day. "This is more effective for me than asking, 'When is the best time to contact you?'" he says. "That ends my flexibility, and then I have to plan my day around that three P.M. call.

"Since I deal with various industries, I need to understand how my prospect's day is structured in each and every business. Overall, I want to catch my prospect during the least stressful time of day. I find the most successful time of the week for prospecting is Friday mornings (not late afternoon). People are happy on Friday, knowing that the weekend is almost upon them, so they tend to have a better attitude."

There is no perfect time to catch a customer. Some salespeople don't like to call on prospects on Monday morning because it seems to be a busy time for everyone. But I've made some of my best contacts then. People are usually in first thing on Monday, cleaning up any weekend messes, and are anxious to make sure the ship gets turned around and headed in the right direction.

The best time to reach someone depends on the individual, the business he's in, and his particular routine. That's why it's important to ask people, especially the first time you talk to them, what is the best time to call. Note it down on your

"The average person puts only 25 percent of his energy and ability into his work. The world takes off its hat to those who put in more than 50 percent of their capacity, and stands on its head for those few and far between souls who devote 100 percent."

—ANDREW CARNEGIE

contact sheet or in your computer. Use your voice-mail message to help you pin people down by including the sentence "Please leave the best day and time for me to get back to you." That way, you can eliminate some of the inevitable phone-tag time.

Don't forget to keep yourself in the timing equation, too. Sometimes, it's not as important to try to figure out if this is a good time to call the customer as it is to say, "How 'up' am I right now?" If you're in a bad mood, if you're not excited and enthusiastic, you may not do as good a selling job as when you've got your own juices flowing.

[Focus *on* *the* Big Picture]

It's easy to get overwhelmed by the amount of work ahead of you. Most salespeople juggle many accounts at once and are always in the process of adding more. And with every new account come added tasks and responsibilities, the follow-up, the paperwork. This growing mountain of tasks can be frustrating and stressful, and when you get stressed, it's much more difficult to work smart. That's the time to take a step back and make sure you're seeing the big picture, as well as focusing on all the little steps to get you there. That means creating a focal point—a goal or a series of goals—that is clear and sharply defined, keeping that point in mind throughout the workday, and weeding out the things that distract you. It means setting priorities for each day, and then taking one step at a time to meet them.

Here are ten ideas to help you clear your head, set priorities, and get done what you need to get done.

1. Make a daily list of things to do and people to call.

Make the list long enough so that it's a challenge to get to all of them in a day, but not so long that it's physically impossible. Prioritize your tasks, then start with number one, concentrating solely on what has to be accomplished in that call, and when you've gone as far as you can, move on.

2. Don't skip over the small steps.

The only way to accomplish anything is to go step by step. I'm not a particularly patient person, and when I started Tae Kwon Do, all I could see was that people seemed to be practicing the same moves over and over again. I asked my teacher, "How do I learn if I do the same thing every time I come here?" He told me that you learn only by practicing and mastering one small step at a time, and though it may not seem like progress to you, every day you improve. Every time you practice, you evaluate what you've learned and how you can do it better.

It's the same in business. We have to do the small things in order to accomplish the larger. Whenever people fail in sales, or in any profession, it's usually because they have stopped taking the basic steps—like making cold calls and keeping in touch with current clients—that are the foundation for sales success. But the most successful salespeople know that it is when we skip over those little things that everything else becomes massively difficult.

3. Focus.

Stay in the moment. Think about what you have to accomplish at the moment you're doing it. You can reflect upon the past and dream about the future when the project is completed, but while it's under way keep your focus sharp and to the point. When your attention drifts, your tenacity falters and you lose sight of your goals.

4. If you're knocked down, get back up.

No matter how many times you're felled, get up again. That's the key to success. You can't let the setbacks get to you personally, inside. People may tell you "it can't be done." Sometimes, all that means is that *they* couldn't do it. Don't let other people's thoughts make you think differently. When you're knocked down, get back up again no matter how much you or your pride has been hurt. You never know what may happen the next time.

5. Can't get through the door? Try the window.

If the window is locked, go down the chimney. Look for every opening. Try every single possibility. Don't give up because the one way you've tried is blocked. There are many paths that lead to the same destination. As Henry Wadsworth Longfellow said, "If you only knock long enough and loud enough at the gate, you are sure to wake somebody up."

6. Ask for help.

There is a romantic image we all have of the rugged individual, the one who blazes new paths relying only on his or her own stubborn strength. That is a romantic fantasy. There's no reason to do everything yourself. There are lots of people around you who will be more than willing to help. Some may turn you down. Some may not believe in you or your dreams. Ignore them! Find those out there who can lend you support, whether it be physical, financial, or emotional. The tenacity of a team multiplies the tenacity of the individual.

7. Be patient.

There are things in life that may take time for us to achieve. Keep the body, mind, and heart focused. I've been working on a project for seven years, and only now is it becoming a reality. Of course, this was not the only project I had during these seven years. Still, I never gave up on this particular dream. Sometimes, the old adage "Slow and steady wins the race" is the way the world works. It takes both courage and patience to keep going when a goal seems unattainable, but that's how the greatest rewards are gained.

8. Be adaptable.

Everyone in business knows that no matter how carefully you plan your day, there will be times when an unexpected crisis arises (a customer's order didn't arrive on time and you have to stop what you're doing and trace the shipment), or a new opportunity presents itself (you're with a client who says, "I think John Jones at Midland Manufacturing could really use your services—let me give him a call and see if he can meet with you right now"). When such situations arise, you have to attend to them. Work far enough ahead on your projects so that if you have to take time out to deal with an unexpected situation, you're not thrown into a crisis mode yourself.

9. Don't just sit there—do something.

Go. Make a phone call. Write a letter. Move things forward. You can theorize all you want, but there's nothing like being in the thick of it to teach you the lessons you need to learn. Don't be afraid to get into the trenches, to take some risks and try new things. Know that at some point you'll probably get "beat up." You don't have to go out looking for a fight, but you have to face the blows when they come. And you have to know, especially when your opponent is bigger and stronger than you are, that you have it in you to go one more round. You may be defeated, but the next time you step into the ring, you'll be a much better fighter.

10. Keep the faith.

Author Simone Weil once said, "Even if our efforts of attention seem for years to be producintg no result, one day a light that is in exact proportion to them will flood the soul." Even when it seems like you'll never achieve your goals, keep believing in yourself. You cannot give any job your best effort unless you believe in what you're doing and continue to have faith, even through hard times. To put it another way, when you go after Moby Dick, bring the tartar sauce. Think of the rewards that will come your way once you accomplish your goal.

CHAPTER RECAP:
THE HARDER YOU WORK,
the LUCKIER YOU GET

$$\left[\begin{array}{c} \textit{Luck is a reward for the hard work} \\ \textit{you've put in to reach your goal.} \\ \textit{You don't just get lucky—you earn it.} \end{array} \right]$$

Hard work brings benefits.

- It makes you feel good.
- It affects your attitude.
- It provides added value to your customers.
- It's an insurance policy for you and for your customers.

It's not how hard you work, it's how smart you work.

- Hard work alone doesn't guarantee success.
- Working smart is the ability to do a task, evaluate it, and see how that task can be done better next time.
- For one week, keep a journal of what you're doing every hour that you're working, then compare that week's activity to the week before.
- Determine how and when you work best—tap into your own body rhythms.

Take advantage of the new technology.

- Automate tasks you don't have time to do.
- Make information accessible throughout the company.
- But don't rely solely on technology—combine the art and science of sales.

Timing is everything.

- Keep calling, faxing, and writing prospects and customers with new information that is of value to them.
- Accommodate your schedule to your customers' whenever possible.
- Keep yourself in the timing equation—make more calls when you've got your own juices flowing.

Focus on the big picture.

- Clear your head, set priorities, and get things done.
  1. Make a daily list of things you have to do, people you have to call.
  2. Don't skip over the small steps.
  3. Focus; stay in the moment.
  4. Get back up each time you get knocked down.
  5. Can't get through the door? Try a window.
  6. Ask for help.
  7. Be patient and persistent.
  8. Be adaptable.
  9. Don't just sit there—do something.
  10. Keep the faith.

6 Fail *to* Plan, Plan *to* Fail

N ot long ago, while walking through the sales department of a client's office, I noticed a huge banner hanging on the wall that said: "The most important thing about a goal is having one." Talk about simplicity.

Dreams and wishes become reality when we set goals for our-selves. The great motivator Napoleon Hill said that "a goal is a dream with a deadline." Goals give us direction and focus. They break down impossible undertakings into achiev-able tasks. They help us keep our vision clear and our footing steady.

> *"You must have long-range goals to keep you from being frustrated by short-range failures."*
>
> —CHARLES C. NOBLE

If you study high achievers in any field, you will find that they have clearly articulated goals that they are constantly striving to achieve. What's more, they don't sit back and rest once a goal has been met; instead, it inspires them to go on and make the next goal that much more challenging.

We all need not only to have goals, but also to write them down, to keep them in mind, to take the daily actions necessary to reach them. We need short-term goals like making a particular number of cold calls each day, and long-term goals like reaching a particular dollar amount of sales or breaking into a specific number of large accounts within a year. There are three important reasons for setting clear goals.

1. Goals help us focus.

The brain is an amazing organ. It allows us to handle many tasks and solve many problems at the same time. However, it can also get easily overwhelmed. The best way to avoid that sense of confusion and loss of focus is to keep your mind working toward specific goals. When your goals are clearly delineated, your mind is working toward them all the time, whether you know it or not. It's like trying to remember a name—it pops into your head hours later, when you're no longer thinking about it. Your brain has been subconsciously working on this memory for hours, making neurological connections that eventually feed into your conscious mind to say, "You wanted to know this person's name? Here it is!" The same thing happens with goals. Once you write them down and begin to take actions toward them, the subconscious mind is constantly aware of them. Often, when you least expect it, your brain will send a message: "You wanted to work toward that goal? Here's something that will help you get there. . . ." You suddenly start to tap into those "lucky" opportunities all around you to help you achieve your goal.

2. Goals drive us forward.

I believe we have an innate need to achieve and that we're at our best when we work toward achieving a worthy goal. A worthy goal is something that you believe in, something that challenges you. The easiest way to avoid letting the tough times get you down is always to have some goal you're working toward that keeps you excited. Success is built on a strong sense of purpose, on our belief in and passion for the goals we set. We need goals that are set high. We don't need to set impossible goals, but we do need to amaze ourselves—and we have the capacity to do that every single day.

Think of yourself twenty-five years from now. Will you look back and think, "I could have done more"? Or will you recognize that hunger and desire inside yourself and let it lead you to a goal you thought was beyond your abilities? As Kramer on *Seinfeld* once said, "Wouldn't it be hell if someday God showed you what you could have done with your life?"

The most successful people keep asking themselves, "Where am I now, and where do I want to go?" They keep working toward a goal, and once they achieve it, they set new, and higher, goals.

It's been said that when the astronauts who went to the moon came back to Earth, they suffered from anxiety, depression, and other emotional problems. Why? Because they spent years preparing for their mission and then . . . what do you do after you've gone to the moon? They had reached their ultimate goal and no longer had anything to strive toward. It's a lesson to remember: No objective is so great that it is the be-all and the end-all. We must always be setting the bar a little higher, reaching for another goal.

3. Reaching a goal increases our confidence for reaching the next goal.

That's because success breeds success. Every step you take toward achieving your goal teaches you a lesson you can apply to your next goal. The greatest lesson of all is one of the most clichéd: What the mind can conceive and believe it can achieve. Have faith in your ideas, have faith in your abilities, and you are already more than halfway there.

[Living *in the* Real World]

Be careful to set your goals within the realm of possibility. It's sometimes difficult to know where the boundaries lie. If you've never played soccer in your life, and you're now over fifty, you probably won't be able to make the World Cup soccer team.

You might, however, be able to interest other adults in forming a league, and train to win local or regional meets. Your first goals would have to be about getting yourself into shape, forming a team, then forming a league, then improving your team's performance. . . . Each one of those goals would stretch you further than the one before, yet each would be possible to reach.

Setting realistic goals is something that Gene Salerno, general manager of the Perrier Group of America, learned about at an early age. When Salerno was a young man, he used to accompany his father to the racetracks at Suffolk Downs, Aqueduct, Freehold, and Atlantic City—not to place bets, but to sell animal health products to the trainers and owners.

> *"You don't have to be a fantastic hero to do certain things— to compete. You can be just an ordinary chap, sufficiently motivated to reach challenging goals."*
>
> —SIR EDMUND HILLARY

"My dad and I used to have daily, weekly, and monthly goals," says Salerno. "We'd add them up, which would help us pace ourselves so that we wouldn't be overwhelmed. Every day, we knew what we were trying to achieve. It also helped us manage our day, because we knew how much time we had and who we had to see in order to achieve our goal. It really helped us focus.

"Sometimes, I think people have the wrong idea about

setting goals. First, they set too many. And, second, they set unrealistic goals. There's a difference between being unrealistic and being a stretch. In order to keep your goals realistic, you have to know that you'll have small wins along the way."

Don Fink of Citicorp Private Bank has put that same philosophy into what he calls the "one percent improvement" plan. The idea for one percent improvement came to him when he began running marathons. He spent three years placing in the middle of the pack. Then he decided he wanted to break into the top three, to hear his name announced and be awarded his medal in front of the cheering crowd. He trained harder than ever, and in his next race came in eighth.

At first, he was satisfied because he had, after all, moved up from the middle of the pack to the top ten finishers. But then a few weeks later he read the actual race results and times. The person who had come in third, which had been Fink's goal, finished the race one minute and forty seconds before Fink. Doing the math, Fink realized that the third-place winner was only one percent faster than he was.

"I remember asking myself, 'Can I become one percent faster?'" he says. "I thought for a few seconds and then answered, 'Of course I can!'"

It is this one percent factor that changes a dream into an achievable goal. It may be too great a leap to set a goal of moving from the middle of the pack to third place in one fell swoop. But it's not too great to focus on the steps necessary to improve that tiny increment of one percent.

Don Fink has used the one percent improvement concept many times since that race to help him stay focused and motivated. "Every time I found a 'one percent improvement,' then and only then would I focus on where to find my next 'one percent improvement,'" he says. "Ask yourself right now, 'Can I perform one percent better at my job?' 'Can I be a one percent better husband or wife?' 'Can I be a one percent better person?' If the answer is yes to any of these questions, write down a list of all the ways you can think of to achieve a one percent improvement. Then pick a couple of items from your list and go to work on them."

On the other hand, some of your goals should be ones you're not sure you can achieve. You wouldn't make a goal of becoming an Olympic shot-putter within a year. That's not possible. But you can set goals that are within the realm of what you're interested in, yet are beyond what you think you can do. When you do that, you'll be amazed at the power of just setting these goals, and you'll probably find you've gone further than you ever thought possible.

[Be Specific About Your Goals]

One of the reasons high achievers are able to successfully meet their goals is that they are very specific about the targets they set. If a goal is vague and/or ambiguous, it's hard to know whether you've reached it. For instance, suppose your goal is "to become a better salesperson." What does that mean? How do you define "better"? How will you know when you get there?

The path to accomplishment starts in the mind, travels into the word, and is completed through physical action. It's far easier to reach a goal if you can break it down into concrete steps. Following are two basic methods many successful people use to keep them moving toward their goals—they visualize their goals and they make their goals visible.

1. *Visualize your goals.*

Visualization is more than daydreaming; it's seeing a whole step-by-step process in your mind, from beginning to end. Athletes use this process all the time. Runners picture an entire race, planning how and when they will pace themselves and when they will put on that extra burst of energy to cross the finish line. In his book *Golf My Way,* Jack Nicklaus explained that he visualizes his swings backward, visualizing the outcome and then coming back to fill in the steps: "First I 'see' the ball where I want it to finish, nice and white and sitting up high on the bright green grass. Then . . . I 'see' the ball going there; its path, trajectory . . . even its behavior on landing. Then . . . the next scene shows me making the kind of swing that will turn the previous images into reality."

It doesn't matter whether you start from the beginning and move toward the desired outcome, or start with the outcome and then see the steps that got you there. What does matter is that you go through the steps. See yourself being successful at each one, and you're likely to reach a successful conclusion.

2. *Make your goals visible.*

I call my office the "war room." It's a physical representation of everything I need and want to accomplish. I'm a visual person, and I work best, and get the most done, when I can see my tasks and goals literally looming large in front of me. So I have giant white boards on my walls where I can organize (and reorganize) both my long- and short-term goals. Everywhere I look, I can see where I want to go and what I'm trying to achieve. Even when I'm traveling, I can close my eyes and see the goals posted on my walls.

The other day, I was working in my office, trying to juggle several projects at once, when I suddenly became overwhelmed. What helped me out that day (and on many other days) was the fact that my goals literally appeared before my very eyes. I realized that some of my goals had changed; some of my priorities had changed. I rewrote my goals so that they reflected these changes. Because I really had to think about reworking these goals, it helped me focus. Soon I was much calmer, and once again I knew exactly what I wanted.

Every time I look at my goal boards, they channel me and pull me forward. They also help me live in the moment. My goals point me toward the future, but they let me know that there are things I have to *do* today. Goals don't achieve themselves. When I remind myself of my goals, I stop and think,

"What do I need to do today to move closer to them?" I even have the word *today* posted on one of the boards to remind me not to get caught up in reliving past mistakes or in getting so involved in tomorrow's possibilities that I don't focus on what needs to be done right now.

You can set up a war room of your own—a space where you can look around and with one glance know what you've already accomplished and what's left to be done. It should be a place where you know you "mean business." As you look around, you can say, "Here's what needs to be done today." This is the place to gather yourself together and get things done.

There are all kinds of goals you might want to set, and you can hang up as many goal boards as your walls can hold. You might want to have separate boards for financial goals, activity goals, reading and learning goals. This doesn't mean you spend all your time setting up goal boards. My office walls are covered with boards, and I may change one or two items a day. But when you keep your goals visible in front of you, they become part of you, as if by osmosis. They force you to work on the little things that get the big things done.

In some circumstances, you may not want to post your goals where everyone can see them. You could keep them in a notebook that you pull out of your desk every morning and can put away when other people are around. You can post some at home so that you can see them before you get to work. The important thing is to make your goals visible to you as often as possible.

[Whose Goals Are They Anyway?]

Up until now, I've been talking about personal goals. For many salespeople, however, personal goals are only part of the picture. Managers often set goals for you, individually and as a team. Don Fink of Citicorp Private Bank puts his yearly goals up on a poster in his office at the beginning of the year.

"Throughout the year we have various product launches, offerings that come out for a limited period of time," he says. "Then I do what I call 'posting goals.' I actually make up signs and post them in the offices of all the salespeople, letting them know what I expect them to do. I put it in front of them in black and white. It's always going to be something achievable, but something that's also going to be a stretch for them. It's actually kind of fun—everybody knows that a new product means a new goal, but they don't know what the numbers are going to be."

Fink has a computer program that helps him keep track of all the deals his team is working on, the probability of closing, the timing of closing, and what the profitability will be. He looks at that every day and uses it as the basis for planning how he's going to improve performance and get the most out of his people or, as he says, "how to help my people get the most out of themselves."

Fink encourages everyone on his team to write down his or her goals. Everyone is initially enthusiastic about doing it. "But when I ask them, 'Did you do it?' they all say, 'No.' Almost nobody does it. It's because it's a commitment. If they write it down, they're committed to doing it. That means they set themselves up for success or failure, and they're just not comfortable doing that."

For Fink, making a commitment spurs him on. He uses both the fear of failure and the hope of reward to keep both himself and his team motivated. Everyone knows which people on the team are reaching their goals and which people aren't. For those who are, Fink has established the Hunters' Club. There is no reward for being in this club, except that those who are in it earn the respect of everyone else on the team.

Fink communicates daily, weekly, monthly, and yearly goals to his entire team. Higher management in the company determines what his team's numbers should be, but these are not good enough for Fink. "To motivate myself and the people who work for me, I increase my goals," he says. "I personally assign myself and my team higher goals. I meet with them and tell them both the goals we were given and the goals I have set. It tells my team that I think more of them than the senior-level people do, that I have a higher regard for their abilities. I let them know that as a team we're going to set higher standards for ourselves than others do."

$$\left[\begin{array}{c}\textbf{Seven Steps } \textit{to}\\\textbf{Achieving Your Goals}\end{array}\right]$$

It's easy to understand the concepts behind setting achievable goals, but how do you actually do it? Here are seven steps to help you set and meet your goals.

1. Break down your goals.

There is no other way to accomplish a goal except to take it one step at a time. Every high achiever accepts this as truth. We all wish it could be different, that we could just snap our fingers or wiggle our noses and achieve our goals. But goals are achieved only if they are built on the bricks of hard work, one brick at a time. A goal becomes more realistic when you realize you don't have to take a giant step to reach it. One small step at a time will do; the smaller the steps, the easier the climb.

2. Write your top goals on a small piece of paper you can keep in your wallet.

Even if you have a "war room," write down one or two of your most important goals and keep them in your wallet. Most likely, you use your wallet every day, so you'll see your goals before you every day. Goals are often associated with making more money; the more money you make, the more you'll use your wallet. The more you use your wallet, the more often you'll see your goals in front of you.

3. Tell everybody about your goals.

Once you say them out loud, you're committed to them. This doesn't mean you can never change a goal, it's just another external reminder to keep on track. If you do change a goal and people ask you about it, you will have to lay out the reasons for them, which will help you determine whether you made the change for good, sound reasons or just because the original goal was proving difficult to achieve. As the German writer Goethe once said, "The moment one definitely commits oneself, then providence moves too."

4. List all the benefits of achieving your goals.

Even if your goal is based on something you don't like, find reasons you want to accomplish it. If your boss says, "I need that report done by October 15," make a list of the benefits you'll get by doing a great job on the report and completing it on time (or even earlier). Your boss will be impressed. You can remind your boss about this when it comes time for performance review. You'll have a better chance of getting promoted, which will mean more money for you and your family, and so on. Even if you're not excited about the goal itself, you can be passionate about what achieving that goal will do for you.

5. Study past successes.

Look at people who have done the things that you're trying to do. Are there other sales reps in your company who are achieving the kinds of goals you would like to achieve? If so, talk to these people. Ask them what steps they have taken. Study the process they've gone through. Read biographies of successful salespeople and compare what they've done to what the people you speak to in your company have done. These are ideas that have already been tested by the best in the business, so you should be able to find a few that appeal to you and apply them to your own situation.

6. Consult outsiders.

Bounce your idea or goal off someone who is not in your line of work—someone who has no clue about what you're trying to do. Sometimes, a totally fresh perspective from someone who is not jaded by what has not worked in this area before will help you gain insight into what will.

7. Take your own path.

Early in my career I read a wonderful little book called *I Dare You!*, which was written in 1931 by William H. Danforth, founder of the Ralston Purina Company. In one section, Danforth dares his readers to write down their goals for the future. I did this. Recently, I came across my copy of the book, and I reread my goals. The first thing I thought was, "They've all been accomplished!" The second thing I thought was, "Why did I set these goals? They weren't very much of a stretch." But then I remembered how big they were for me then. And how much I've changed since the time I first read this book.

Although you can learn a lot by studying others' success,

you can only achieve your own by following your own path and finding your own way to take the journey of life. Only by daring to be yourself and to have confidence in your own abilities can you achieve greatness. "The only reason you are not the person you should be is you don't dare to be," says Danforth. "Once you dare, once you stop drifting with the crowd and face life courageously, life takes on a new significance. New forces take shape within you. New powers harness themselves for your service."

So Many Goals, So Little Time

Often, the problem with setting goals is that you have to find the time to work toward them. In our activity-laden busy lives, we're always searching for ways to manage our time. To many people, time management means segmenting their lives (especially their work lives) into little boxes, each box representing a certain number of minutes or hours. To me, time management means putting things in perspective. Think about the 4.5 billion years the earth has been in existence. Think about the seventy-plus years the average person spends on Earth. Put into that perspective, we are here for the blink of an eye. We have much to accomplish in such a brief time.

Time management is learning to appreciate the value of

every moment you have on Earth. Not every moment will be earth-shattering. There will be moments of excitement, moments of depression, and quiet moments of introspection. But no moment should go to waste. You can't plan every moment of your life. But you can look at how you spend your moments, and think about whether or not you are spending your time wisely—and, if not, find ways to make necessary changes.

Managing time effectively means more than keeping a schedule and marking a calendar. It means being careful with your time, not careless. It means making value judgments about what you do at work and at home. It means making the choice to spend your time with people you care about. It means having a greater awareness of the world around you and your place in it.

Managing your time is impor-

> *"He who every morning plans the transactions of the day and follows out that plan, carries a thread that will guide him through the labyrinth of the most busy life."*
>
> —*VICTOR HUGO*

tant to sales in the same way it's important in any successful endeavor. You start out by defining your objective and what you're trying to accomplish, and then you figure out the best way to make it happen. If you set up your goals, decide what tactics you're going to use, and then plan out your time in an efficient way, you will achieve the desired results.

Time is the most precious commodity there is. Those who don't plan how they're going to use their time, and just let the day happen to them, accomplish the least.

The first step in managing your time is to take a few days and analyze how you're spending your time. Every time you undertake an activity, ask yourself, "Is this time expenditure appropriate for me? Can it be eliminated? What would happen if I stopped doing this?" Maybe it's something that can be delegated to someone else.

Take voice mail, for instance. If you sit and listen to your voice messages, you could spend half an hour just writing them down. On the other hand, perhaps you can have an assistant listen to the messages, then type them up for you, including names and phone numbers. Then you can go through them in just a few minutes. It's a task that needs to be done, but not necessarily by you.

Think about how you handle your e-mail. E-mail has not replaced the letter or the phone call; it is an add-on. Of course, it has its good points, but we somehow feel we are at the mercy of our e-mail—that we have to pay attention to it at all times. People will call and say, "Did you get the e-mail I sent you fifteen minutes ago?" The solution is to think of your e-mail as being delivered like your paper mail, and that you will check it only at a specific time. The idea that you must send an instant response is damaging to your work and your life.

The way you manage your time depends on your own temperament. Some people find it confusing and overwhelming to have to keep many balls in the air at the same time. Others are energized by that situation. Just remember that no matter how many projects you have, you can concentrate on only one thing at a time.

David Allen, a business expert, once said, "You can do anything, but you can't do everything." What that means is that you can do it all, but you can't do it all at the same time. You have to acknowledge that you are a human being with human limitations. You have to take everything in sequence. Write down the sequence and say, "I'll do this task first—it should take me this long—then I'll do the next one." Otherwise, it's like gridlock with everybody trying to cross the intersection at the same time. No one goes anywhere. It's all about setting up a sequence of priorities. It's common sense, but it's difficult to think about when you're caught in the fray. That's why you need to make it a habit in your life.

[A Tool *for* You]

It doesn't really matter what method you use for your goal-setting, planning, or time management. Some people use computerized systems; some people use their goal boards; and some people have Post-it notes stuck all over their desks. Any one of these systems may work perfectly for you. But none of them works perfectly for everyone. Every high achiever I've met has an individual system that he or she has devised to help manage time. Some are complicated; some are as simple as a little black book. The system you use is less important than using a system that works for you.

The ultimate goal of all our lives is to be happy and fulfilled. Goal-setting is simply a tool we can use to help us on our way. There's no need to overwhelm yourself by setting too many goals at once. Work on one at a time; then, as soon as you are nearing one destination, you can begin planning for the next journey. And it's most important to remember that whether or not you reach your goal is less important than knowing you did your best to work toward it. Goals should be chosen with great care and concern. Be prepared to get what you go after. Whatever it is that you really want can be achieved if you write it on the page and engrave it in your mind.

CHAPTER RECAP:
FAIL *to* PLAN, PLAN *to* FAIL

[
*Goals give us direction and focus;
they break down impossible undertakings
into achievable tasks, and they help us keep
our vision clear and our vision steady.*
]

Three reasons for setting clear goals:

1. Goals help us focus.
2. Goals move us forward.
3. Reaching a goal increases your confidence for reaching the next goal.

Living in the real world.

- Don't set goals so high that they are unattainable.
- Use the one percent improvement plan.
  - Focus on the steps it would take to improve by a tiny increment of one percent.

Be specific.

- Visualize your goals.
- Make your goals visible.

Whose goals are they anyway?

- If you are setting goals for others, set them high enough to be a stretch.
- Make a commitment to your goals by writing them down.

Seven steps to achieving your goals:

1. Break down goals into small steps.
2. Write down your goals on a small piece of paper you can keep in your wallet.
3. Tell everybody about your goals.
4. Write down all the benefits of achieving your goals.
5. Study past successes.
6. Consult the clueless—bounce your ideas off people who are not in your line of work.
7. Follow your own path.

So many goals, so little time.

- Time management means learning to appreciate the value of every moment you have on Earth.
- Look at how you spend your moments, and think about whether or not you are spending your time wisely.
- Define your objective, then figure out the best way to make it happen.
- Analyze how you currently spend your time.

7 It's Not WHAT You Know, It's WHO You Know

A while back, I was working with the president of a company who told me that one of his goals was to get large national accounts for his business. At the time, I was hosting a syndicated radio program on achievement. Many of my guests were founders and CEOs of large national companies, as were many of my own customers. So I saw several opportunities to introduce these executives to the president I was working with. Some he ended up doing business with, others he did not. But the president of the first company is now someone I can rightfully call and ask, "Do you know anyone else who might benefit from my service?"

Selling should be a win-win situation. If you help your customers build their businesses, they will not hesitate to help you build yours. Keep your eye on your network, and when you see a good match, put the two together. Once you've shown your customers you're willing to make an effort for them, you can ask for something in return. As Zig Ziglar once said, "You can get everything you want out of life if you just help enough other people get what they want."

Most salespeople have heard that cliché. Zig Ziglar may have put it in those words, but it's really a very old philosophy. It's the Golden Rule: "Do unto others as you would have them do unto you." It's in the Bible: "As you sow, so shall you reap." But how many of us practice this philosophy when we're networking? We think that networking means we have to go out and promote ourselves. Sure, it's good to get your name (and/or product) out in front of the buying public. It certainly can't hurt for you to join civic organizations and become known in the community. And it can only do you good to become an expert in your field, sought after to give speeches and quoted in newspapers and magazines.

> *"Personal relationships are the fertile soil from which all advancement, all success, all achievement in life grows."*
>
> —BEN STEIN

But that's only a small part of networking. The largest part of networking is going out to help someone else. Then, when you need referrals, the people you've helped will be glad to bring you into their circle of contacts. Not only that, knowing that you helped them out in their time of need, they'll recommend you so highly to other potential customers that the sale will already be made for you.

[Leveraging Your Success]

Most salespeople are natural-born networkers. If we didn't truly enjoy connecting with people, we wouldn't be salespeople. Networking is both a skill and an art, and it takes practice to make it work for you.

We all have a circle of people we know, made up of family, friends, colleagues, acquaintances, and customers. In a perfect world, we could keep selling to the same people over and over again and still make our quota. But even if that were possible, it wouldn't be very challenging or stimulating, nor would it help to expand a business. It's only by forming an ever-widening circle of contacts that you can keep your business growing.

Networking means using the people within your circle to help you expand it. You do that by helping develop relationships between two or more people. For instance, if I introduce one person to another, I try to improve the relationship between these two people at the same time that I'm improving my relationship with each of them. These links must be beneficial to all concerned parties, even if one benefits immediately and the others benefit later. If there is no mutual benefit, it is not networking.

The ultimate goal of networking is to have satisfied customers and reputable business people (other than yourself) urging other people to do business with you. Then you are, in effect, building a sales force of people who are helping you build your business.

That's why networking is so much more than just exchanging business cards with a group of strangers. Going to networking clubs and social events is one way to meet people and widen your circle of acquaintances, but it's not the most efficient way to network for business.

Beverly Hyman is a consummate networker. In fact, she has networked her way into building one of the most successful organizational development and training firms in the country, Beverly Hyman and Associates. "When the playwright John Guare wrote *Six Degrees of Separation*, he hypothesized that everyone was only six people from contacting any other person in the world," says Hyman. "I think there are

> *"You can succeed best and quickest by helping others to succeed."*
>
> —NAPOLEON HILL

really only two or three degrees, if you network well." And net-working, she says, can be divided into four useful categories.

1. Leapfrogging.

This is when you follow people on and off through life. "For instance," says Hyman, "twenty-five years ago I did some work for a man at Time, Inc. He left that job and went to the American Management Association. I did work for him there. I have continued to sell him my services throughout his career—and now he is head of training and development for an organi-zation that has ninety thousand employees." Leapfrogging also includes networking within an organization, so that if your con-tact leaves, you keep your relationship with his or her "old" company while making inroads into the "new" company.

2. Chance encounters.

You never know where you may meet your next business con-tact, Hyman believes. Keep your eyes, ears, and mind open wherever you are—whether it's at a convention, on an airplane, or standing in line at the post office.

3. Stepping outside your narrow circle.

There's no point in constantly trying to network within the same narrow confines. You've got to keep putting yourself outside your safe, familiar circle. "I volunteered to do some work for the literacy movement a few years ago," says Hyman. "I didn't know anybody within that organization. But I met people there. One man on the board introduced me to someone at the Weizmann Institute of Science. Someone there introduced me to someone at the United Jewish Federation. And so on and so on. I now do work for all of these organizations—through connections I made by stepping outside of my usual circle of contacts."

4. Putting other people together.

Do someone else a favor, and it will come back to you tenfold, sooner or later. If you see an opportunity to hook up two people, do so—even if it has no obvious benefit for you. Know someone who's looking for a job? Know someone who's looking for experienced help? Introduce the two to each other. If you know of a company with a problem that you can't solve and you know someone who might be able to provide a solution, put the two together. Eventually, they'll both remember your good deed. And when they need the type of product or service you provide, your phone will start ringing.

[Networking *for* New Business]

There are, of course, other ways of networking than connecting two of your contacts. There is the more classic form of networking that many people use, especially when they are starting out in business.

Jeanne Quagliano of the Perrier Group tells about a salesperson who came to work for her right out of college. "She made a list of everyone she knew in her life who might have a use for our product," says Quagliano. The young woman organized her list into friends, friends' parents, her neighbors, her relatives, merchants in the town, the school she graduated from, and the church she attended. She started out talking to the people within her closest circle of contacts. She asked each of them if they could use her service. Then she asked if they could give her the names of five other people to call.

"Before we knew it, this young woman was averaging fifty new customers a month. And our goal was only twenty-five!" says Quagliano. "Not only that, she continued her networking throughout the company. Some of the names she got were outside her territory, so she passed those leads over to other salespeople. Then she followed up with them to make sure they had followed up on her lead. She

> *"Networking is just a matter of common sense. No one person can possibly know everything or everyone they need to know. If you're there for other people, most people are happy to help when you need it."*
>
> —RIEVA LESONSKY

wasn't getting credit for the sales; she was thinking of the good of the whole division.

"Networking means being attuned to who you're meeting in all sorts of circumstances, whether it's in business, while you're traveling, or in your personal life. All of these are opportunities to share ideas with people—to find out what they have to offer and what you can offer them."

[The Art *of* Getting Referrals]

People who are satisfied with your product and service can be the best kind of advertising you'll ever encounter. But unless you ask them to, they won't necessarily think of spreading the word about your worth around. And many salespeople are reluctant to ask. They say, "My customer has just given me business and now I'm asking him for more business from somebody else? I can't do it."

You can do it, if you feel you've earned it. If you believe in the value of your product or service and your value as a salesperson, then you have the right to ask. You're not really asking for more business; you're asking for the opportunity to help solve someone else's problems.

Here are several techniques for getting and making the most of referrals.

❏ **Get feedback from your customers.** You don't just want to make a sale; you want to form a relationship. You want that relationship to result in repeat business and in recommendations to others. So keep tabs on how you're doing with your customers. Ask your customers for their opinions, and they'll probably be glad to tell you. Call and ask, "Is there anything we're not doing that we should be?" Or send them a brief survey to fill out about how you and your product or service are performing. This will give you a chance to correct any problems you may uncover, and you can use positive surveys as a referral tool for prospective clients ("Here's a survey we conducted with Acme Manufacturing, and you can see how satisfied they were with our product and service").

❏ **Get your customers to sell for you.** How does a prospect you've never met before know that you are sincere and trustworthy? You can talk all you want about how wonderful your product is and how great your follow-up will be. But the most convincing evidence you can produce is testimony from other satisfied customers. After customers buy, interview them about why they purchased from you and what benefits they've enjoyed from your product or service. Ask them to write you a testimonial letter. Most satisfied customers will gladly do this. Then you can put several letters together into a portfolio of your success. (Don't forget to thank your customers for their testimonials with a handwritten letter of gratitude.)

❑ **Ask for a referral right after a success.** When is the best time to ask for a referral? When you've just delivered something the customer is pleased with—when you've solved a problem, followed through on a promise, or helped the client in some other way. In other words, when you've earned his trust and respect and given him reason to believe you will do the same for others. That's when your relationship is at its strongest, and people are most willing to recommend you to others. When is the worst time to ask for a referral? Never asking at all is the worst choice. Obviously, you have to pick and choose whom you ask and when, but even on a cold call you can ask, "Is there anyone else you know of in the area who could benefit from our service?"

❑ **Use referrals to get into large accounts.** When you're dealing with large accounts, being referred in is often what gets you your first appointment. The three most useful referral sources are:

1. People outside the organization who can refer you to people in the organization.

2. People inside the organization who can refer you to other people in the organization.

3. People from other accounts who can testify to the quality of your service or product.

If you don't know anyone offhand who can refer you, study the company's annual report. Look at the board of directors, the law firm, the accountants, any names that may be familiar to you. These people may be able to introduce you to people within the organization who can help you directly or send you in the right direction. Most sales reps don't realize that it takes only a few seconds to ask a question like "Would you know of two or three other people who might benefit from our service?" Small accounts may be able to refer you to the larger accounts. Large accounts may have other divisions that can use your services.

❏ **Think of ways to help your customer's business grow.** Help your customer in any way you can—whether or not it has anything to do with the sale of your product. You might be in a position to get your customer some publicity, or you might know someone who is able to help them out of a jam (even if that someone is your competition). Whatever you can do to help your customer's business will help yours as well; the more you help them out, the more likely they will be to refer you to others.

❑ **Once you get a referral, learn all you can about the new prospect.** Don't just call and say, "Mr. Smith recommended I call you," and go into a presentation. Do your homework first. Read up on the company, check its Web site, and when you call, ask qualifying questions. You might say, "Mr. Smith recommended I call. He speaks very highly of you and thought you might be able to benefit from my product the way he did. But before I tell you about my product, I'd like to find out a little bit about you."

❑ **Thank customers for their referrals—even if they don't work out.** A customer might expect you to say thanks if you make a sale on her recommendation. But even if the sale doesn't go through, be sure to show your appreciation. Then the customer might be willing to give you other referrals down the line.

[Networking *for* Advice]

There are other reasons for networking, besides making sales. One of the best reasons is to get advice from those whom you trust and respect. We all need teachers and mentors, people we can turn to for objective opinions, guidance, recommendations, contacts—and referrals.

Many people are afraid to ask for help. We think we have to do everything on our own, or it is a sign of weakness. But if you look closely at people who have made it to the top, they have rarely done it alone. All successful people realize that they have areas of weakness, and they are not shy about finding others with more knowledge and/or experience. The president of the United States has an entire cabinet of people he can turn to for advice whenever he needs it. Professional athletes have coaches, agents, and managers. And most company presidents and CEOs have a strong staff of people under them, along with peers and colleagues they turn to in times of need.

> *"He that walketh with wise men shall be wise . . ."*
>
> —THE BIBLE, PROVERBS 13:20

You can't sit around and wait for others to help you—take action and you will find the help you need. Successful people know what their strengths are, and they know they have to depend on others to bolster their weaknesses. They are not shy about asking for help when they need it.

So how do you go about cultivating mentors? Here are a few hints:

Begin by making a list of people you can call for help and advice. Call a few people who have a background in the industry you're trying to penetrate, and some others who have an outsider's point of view. Call as many people as you can and say, "I wonder if you can help me out. Here's my situation. Here's what I know so far and what's already occurred. If you were in my position, what would you do next?" Take notes, and list the key ideas each person has given you.

Keep an open mind about the answers you get. You may not agree with everything you're told. It's sometimes easier for other people to see things we are unable to see, so don't dismiss someone's advice or opinion without giving it careful study. You may even get contradictory advice from various people you call, and you'll have to use your own judgment to decide what will work best for you.

Be persistent; if you want to reach a particular person, keep trying. High achievers are often available, but they're always busy. It may take many tries before you ever reach the person. On the other hand, most will be enthusiastic about giving back to someone who doesn't give up. After all, that's how they made it.

Make sure you know what you're looking for from the person you contact. Be specific about what you want to know. Write down any questions you might have. Don't just sit back and wait for words of wisdom to change your life; let your prospective mentor know how you think he or she might be able to help. Then ask your potential mentor how you can be of help to him or her. Volunteer to work on a special project. Join trade associations, get on committees, do your fair share. Come up with specific plans of action and ask your mentor for advice and suggestions. And, of course, be sure to send each person who helps you a personal note just to say thanks for their time and feedback.

Remember that most people like to be asked for their advice or their opinion, and most are more than happy to pass on what they've learned. They're flattered to be asked. Nonetheless, you can't expect that everyone you call will be able to give you the help you need. Just remember that everybody is busy, and accommodate their schedules. Most people are willing to take some time out of their busy schedules to share the benefits of their wisdom and experience.

I believe very strongly in the power of mentors. Here are nine important points to remember about them.

1. Find mentors in different areas.

Most people think there is only room for one "great" mentor in their lives. The truth is, there is room for many wise advisers. Some may apply to your business or career, some to your personal life. Find people who are different from each other so that the knowledge you get is not skewed only in one direction.

Walk with people who are thirsty for knowledge. Those are the people you want to be around. Search out people who have a passionate interest in something that interests you. In college, students do internships to learn from experienced elders. This is a practice we should continue throughout life.

2. Find one great person to emulate.

This is not really a contradiction to point number one, although it may seem like it. Among the many mentors you cultivate, find one who is the most respected, the ultimate authority, a genius in his or her field. Ideally, he or she will be someone who has broken the mold in your industry and has come up with amazing and innovative ideas.

3. Plan to surpass your mentor.

Buddha said, "Do not believe what your teacher tells you merely out of respect for the teacher." Don't put your mentor on a pedestal—remember that mentors are human beings, with flaws and faults of their own. So even though you may look up to your mentors, don't let them hold you down. Don't let them argue that theirs is the only way; take the best they have to offer and make it your own. As you grow and learn and expose yourself to new experiences, you may see beyond your mentor's vision.

4. Read biographies.

Role models don't necessarily need to be people we see around us every day. Go back into history and look for those men and women who achieved greatness. Study their lives. Take notes. If something they said or did inspires you, write it down and put it in a spot you will see frequently.

5. Get rid of "antimentors."

Mark Twain once said, "Keep away from people who try to belittle your ambition. Small people always do that, but the really great people make you feel that you, too, can become great." There are some people who are anxious to tell you not what you can do, but what you cannot do. Every time you think of a new idea or new way to go, they tell you you're going in the wrong direction. They try to push you toward their own solution, and then make you feel that your solution was wrong. They say they want to see you grow, but their actions belie their words. Don't let anyone undermine your enthusiasm for growth.

6. Eliminate your own anger, envy, and jealousy.

Sometimes, instead of looking up to those who have more than we do (at the moment), we are jealous of their accomplishments. It's human nature to feel that way. Just don't get stuck in these feelings, because they get in the way of learning. Our own ego puts up barriers to listening to what others have to say. Letting go of that ego allows us to open up and admit that others may have much to contribute. What someone else has never takes away from what you can achieve.

7. Emulate, don't imitate.

Take what your mentors have to give, collect the information they have to pass on, and use it to your benefit. But use it in your own way. Learn from the best, but hold on to your individual uniqueness and style. As Ralph Waldo Emerson said, "Trust thyself; every heart vibrates to that iron string."

8. Revisit greatness.

When you find something or someone that has a message for you—a quote, a book, a special person who infuses you with excitement—return to it again and again. Don't let a great book get dusty on the shelf after you've read it. Don't disregard a mentor after you think you've learned all you can from him or her. Experience and age make many things new again. You are a different person than you were five years ago. Go back to your sources and see what they have to say to you now. Once you go back to a source, it sings to you in a different way. What was valuable before is now even richer and more salient.

9. Become a mentor yourself.

Let others benefit from your skill and knowledge. You'll be amazed at how much you learn as you teach. Every time I do a seminar, I realize that not only am I sharing my knowledge with others, but, more importantly, I'm also refreshing and reminding myself of the basics I sometimes forget. Being a mentor is when you truly learn the most.

What You Know Is Just *as* Important *as* Who You Know

Like all the clichés we've studied so far, this one has its downside. "It's not what you know, it's who you know" is true— in the short term. You can network all you want and get appointments to see all kinds of VIPs, but if you can't deliver for them, they won't be contacts for long. And they certainly won't network you on to further contacts.

You have to know your product. You have to be able to qualify every contact so that you're sure there's a match between their company and what you're selling. You've got to understand what you bring to the table, what makes you different from everyone else offering comparable products or services. You've got to know how to create value for your customers, and then deliver it.

Your goal is to become a credible, reliable resource for your contacts. Then and only then will they feel comfortable urging other people to do business with you.

In July 1999, the *New Yorker* magazine ran an article by James Atlas called "The Million-Dollar Diploma," about people who graduated from Harvard Business School. Basically, it said that the percentage of HBS graduates who are successful is not based so much on the things they learn in class, but on the strength of the network of alumni. Those alumni have an automatic "in" with other graduates. When one 1990 graduate was asked what he'd got out of the school, he replied, "I got a massive number of contacts. It's all about whom you know, whom you trust, who returns your phone calls—or now, e-mail."

Perhaps these graduates do have an initial advantage over those of us who did not go to Harvard. But, I guarantee, if they can't deliver the goods once they get in the door, word will get around that tight-knit network and they will find it even more difficult to make sales than before.

We often hear salespeople complain about these networking advantages. "Of course, she went to Harvard Business School. That's why she gets all those appointments and I can't get any."

According to the complainers, every other salesperson went to a better school, got a better territory, or has an "in" with the manager. They use others' advantages to excuse their own inabilities.

All I know is this: I went to Morris County College, a two-year community college. I don't have a network of well-placed alumni to call upon when I need new business (not that Morris County doesn't have successful alumni—there are many outstanding graduates of the school). But that hasn't stopped me from creating my own network of people I can call upon for referrals.

The bottom line is that when you create a network yourself, built on your excellent reputation, hard work, and credibility, it is much stronger than one you have earned only through educational advantage. Having people recommend you by saying, "You should talk to Bill James—he's trustworthy and capable," is better than having them say, "You should talk to Bill James— he was in my marketing class." A network can break down very easily if there is no leverage behind it.

The best reference you can have is from people who have seen you deliver, who know what you can do. Their confidence in you is then at a high level, and so is their willingness to recommend you to people they know. And since you can't tell which of your customers might have the greatest network on his or her side, you must deliver the same outstanding service to each of them, no matter what the size of the sale. Every customer should be treated as if she were the biggest account you have. You never know who is going to recommend you to whom, so you want to be sure that every customer is getting 100 percent from you.

[Seek, Serve, *and* Sell]

"There's no aspect of business life that I know of that's not dominated by the way we network and interact with other people," says Steve Adubato, Emmy Award–winning television anchor with PBS and author of *Speak from the Heart*. "As competition becomes more and more fierce, the ability to create and maintain strong, viable, long-standing relationships becomes even more critical. It's not just a philosophy, it's a way of life."

The best way to create and maintain those relationships is to seek, serve, and sell.

Seek out the other people's goals and challenges. Find out what's important to them. Figure out the ways that you can serve them by helping them to achieve their goals and meet their challenges. Three things will happen: First, your customers will see you as someone who is willing to help them out when they need it. Second, when it comes time to offer your product or service, you will have a complete understanding of how it will fit their needs. And, third, eventually you will be looked upon as the salesperson of choice. The sale will be the natural extension of an ongoing positive relationship.

CHAPTER RECAP:
IT'S NOT WHAT YOU KNOW, IT'S WHO YOU KNOW

[
Selling should be a win-win situation.
If you help your customers build their business,
they will not hesitate to help you build yours.
]

Leveraging your success.

- Utilize the people within your circle to help you expand it.
- There are four categories of networking:
  1. Leapfrogging.
  2. Chance encounters.
  3. Stepping outside your narrow circles.
  4. Putting other people together.

Networking for new business.

- Contact everyone within your closest circle of friends and acquaintances.
- Ask each of those people to give you the name of five other people to call.

The art of getting referrals.

- If you believe in the value of your product or service and your value as a salesperson, then you have the right to ask for a referral.

- There are several techniques for getting referrals:
  - Get feedback from your customers.
  - Get your customers to sell for you.
  - Ask for a referral right after a success.
- Think of ways to help your customer's business grow.
- Once you get a referral, learn all you can about the new prospect.
- Thank customers for referrals—even if they don't work out.

Networking for advice.

- Don't be afraid to ask for help.
- Cultivate mentors:
  - Make a list of people you can call for help and advice.
  - Use your own judgment to decide if you will take the advice you get.
  - Be selective about the people you approach.
  - Keep trying to reach high achievers.
  - Be specific about what you want to know.
- Nine points to remember about mentors:
  1. Find mentors in different areas.
  2. Find one great person to emulate.
  3. Plan to surpass your mentor.
  4. Read biographies.
  5. Get rid of "antimentors."
  6. Eliminate your own anger, envy, and jealousy.
  7. Emulate, don't imitate.
  8. Revisit greatness.
  9. Become a mentor yourself.

Don't forget what you know when you're looking at who you know.

- If you can't deliver the goods, your contacts won't stay around long.
- Know your product.
- Become a credible, reliable resource for your contacts.
- Build your network based on your reputation, hard work, and credibility.
- Follow your own path.

Seek, serve, and sell.

- Seek out other people's goals and challenges.
- Figure out how to serve them.
- Eventually, you will make the sale.

8 Knowledge Is Power

In the last chapter, I said, "It's not *what* you know, it's *who* you know.'" Now I say, "Knowledge is power." Well, which one is it? It's both. Networking is critical. It gets your foot in the door—but the floor will fall out from under you if you don't have the knowledge to back it up.

> *"Patience and tenacity of purpose are worth more than twice their weight in cleverness."*
>
> —THOMAS HENRY HUXLEY

It seems like common sense: If you want to sell something to someone, you have to know all about it. You have to know what it does, how it works, and how it will benefit a potential customer. These are fundamentals that every salesperson, even the least successful, needs to know.

But what do the most successful salespeople know? They know that their knowledge must take on a much broader scope than mere fundamentals. Facts by themselves do not give you power. It's what you do with those facts—how you apply them—that makes your knowledge powerful.

The more you know, the easier it is to come up with solutions to your customers' problems. That, when you get right down to it, is what selling is all about. And that is what gives you added value, what differentiates you from all the other sales reps selling products or services similar to yours.

When you can find solutions that help your customer run her business better, the customer will see you as a partner in her business, not as someone who stops by every once in a while to sell her something. With today's technology, customers have extensive access to information. They can tap into the Internet, search for "widgets," and gather more facts and figures than they'll ever need. The difficulty is figuring out what information is useful, and what is not. There is nowhere they can turn to on the Net, type in "This is my problem. I know I need a widget, but which widget do I need?," and get an intelligent answer.

That's why they need you. They need you to tell them how your particular widget will help them meet their unique goals and challenges. They may want you to show them how your product or service functions, but they also need you to show them how it can bring value to them. For instance, rather than saying, "Our new widget is thirty percent more powerful than last year's model," you could say, "Our new widget will allow you to produce three hundred more whatchamacallits a month with no increase in overhead." If you have this kind of knowledge, you become a valuable resource to your customers; you become a consultant on how to run their business better.

The most successful salespeople not only are knowledgeable about matters that concern sales, but also have a broader view of the world. Marty Driscoll of Schering Primary Care thinks every rep should read publications like the *New York Times* and the *Wall Street Journal,* along with his or her local paper.

"I believe that everything that happens around you has a potential impact on your customers," he says. "Read your papers. Listen to people. Know that if you're marketing a product in a certain geographic area and the talk is that a major local industry (even if it's not yours) is cutting back employment by fifty percent, that's going to have an impact on many individuals in your territory. It's going to affect their businesses. Conversely, if that industry is expanding by fifty percent, then it's good news for your customers. These are things you must know about."

[Know Your Customer]

If a customer were to ask you, "Why did you choose me?" how would you answer? Would you have to say, "Because you were on my route"? "Because I have to make my quota"? Or could you truthfully say, "Because I know something about you, and what I know tells me that you and my product [or service] are a perfect match"? If you were the customer, which would you rather hear?

We all need to be cared about, and that's how customers feel when a salesperson has taken the time to find out who they are and what they need.

The amount of research you do before you go on sales calls depends on how much time you have and how many calls you have to make. But any information you find out before a meeting can help you develop the right questions to ask during the meeting, and positions you as a knowledgeable "partner" in the customer's business.

Here are some things you might want to find out about a company before you get there:

- The company's history and background
- The company's products and services
- The company's customers
- The company's main competitors
- The company's mission statement

There are many resources you can use to get this type of information:

1. Ask your contacts and mentors.

If you know people in that industry, find out if they can give you any information. You might even know other salespeople who've sold noncompeting products to that company. Recently, I had a meeting scheduled with a VIP in an industry I'd never worked in before. Through my network of contacts, I was able to speak with a high-level executive in another part of that industry, who was more than happy to tell me what he thought would be most important to the VIP. I was able to go into that meeting armed with information I could never have gotten on my own.

2. Use the Internet.

You usually can get a lot of information from a company's Web site (if it has one), including an idea of how the company perceives itself. If the Web site is formal and somewhat intimidating, the corporate culture will probably be that way, too. If the Web site is warm and inviting or has a particular edge to it, you can use those impressions to help plan your presentation. Even if you can't find much information about the company itself on the Internet, you can probably learn a lot about the industry as a whole.

3. Read trade publications.

When you find publications relevant to your prospect's industry, read them to gauge the state of the industry and to learn about the prospect's competitors as well. And don't forget to check out the sections on new product information and on who's been hired or promoted within the industry.

4. Study company literature.

Call the company itself and ask to see any literature it has available, including brochures, catalogs, newsletters, and annual reports. If you're on a long sales cycle, see if you can get on the company's mailing list so that you'll always have updated information.

It's really common sense. A salesperson who has done her homework is a lot more valuable to a customer than someone who hasn't. The client doesn't have to waste time giving the salesperson background information that is easy to obtain elsewhere.

Daniel Berger, a manager for Coca-Cola, knows that understanding his customers' needs sometimes involves doing fieldwork. A few months ago, he had a meeting scheduled with a real estate company that owns 150 buildings nationwide. They were looking to change suppliers for their vending machines. Before the meeting, Berger and his team walked through sixteen of their buildings to identify places they thought machines would have the greatest impact. They were then able to go to the meeting and say, "We've been to your sites. We understand what type of customers you have in your buildings; we have ideas to meet your needs." They were able to make knowledgeable recommendations about how these landlords could best serve their tenants. "We got the sale because we did all our homework and came prepared," says Berger.

[Think *in* Questions]

No matter how much research you do, you'll still need to learn more from your customer to know how to best serve him or her. "Weak salespeople try to close. Great salespeople just ask questions," says author and supreme salesman Hal Becker. "The most important attribute of selling is the part that most salespeople don't understand: that successful salespeople are better at their jobs because they were trained to think in questions." Becker's analogy is to imagine that you are a doctor, and a patient walks into your office for an annual physical. You wouldn't just look at the patient and say, "I think we'll take out your spleen," before you'd even begun an examination. You'd begin by asking a lot of questions to find out whether or not the patient was healthy and, if not, why not.

"A good salesperson will approach you in the same way," says Becker. "He'll go in and find out if the customer has a problem and what he can do to treat it." No matter what the product or service, the questions are basically the same:

- What are you doing now (in terms of this type of product or service)?

- How long have you been doing it?

- Who was your vendor before this one, and why did you switch?

- May I ask what you're presently paying?

- What do you like about your present vendor?

- What don't you like?

- If you could change anything about your present vendor, how would you change it?

For Daniel Berger of Coca-Cola, the object of all these questions is to determine: "What is this customer's buying motive?"

"You can't go in with preconceived notions about why they might want your product," he says. Before Berger was at Coca-Cola, he sold insecticides and herbicides to farmers in South Dakota. Most of them needed his products, but some for different reasons than others.

"Some people wanted to get rid of their weeds so they wouldn't compete with the crops of corn or soybeans," he says. "Other people were more concerned about the aesthetics of their fields, so that their neighbors wouldn't see weeds and think they weren't good farmers. In order to make a sale to any of these farmers, I had to uncover their real motivation for buying my product.

"In the beverage business, it is just as important to understand the customers' needs. Do they want beverages for themselves, for their employees, for their guests? Do they want my product because of the brand or the image? Or is their main reason for buying our product because they like doing business with us?

"Being a district manager, sometimes I'll ride with my salespeople. And what I see them doing (especially when I'm with them) is going out to make a sale. They go in to see a prospect and they're immediately pitching what they want to do and what their ideas are for his account. And they don't even know what the customer needs. So on the next call, I tell them, 'I don't want you to sell a damn thing today. I just want to you sit back and sharpen your pencil and learn what you can offer the customers.' I don't care if they sell a thing on that call."

[Be *a* Consultant]

Alan Boyko of Scholastic Book Fairs sees the sales process from both sides. He sells his books to schools and libraries, and representatives of children's book publishers sell him their books to add to his roster.

"When I think of the best salespeople who call on me, they are the ones who know their business," says Boyko. "But they also know mine. They're really consultants who help me do a better job. For instance, the other day my CFO sat in a meeting with a vendor who was representing a particular publisher. This vendor had an obligation to show us all the books that his company was publishing. But as he was going through his stock, he kept saying, 'You're not going to want this book,' or 'This book isn't for you.' Afterward, the CFO said, 'How does this guy ever sell anything?'"

But Boyko replied, "What do you mean? We're going to do a lot of business with that company!" What the CFO didn't understand was that this salesperson knew his customer. He knew that Scholastic has fairly strict buying criteria, and he wasn't going to try to sell them books they couldn't use.

"Other people leave us every book they have, and it forces my team to read all of those books to find the four or five we really want," says Boyko. "Whereas this 'consultant' said, 'I don't think this book is for you. But you'll love this next book—it has a great story. . . .'"

That sales rep proved to Boyko that he knew and appreciated what Scholastic is all about. "What he presented to me is totally different than what he might present to another customer. He didn't say he didn't like any of the books; he said they weren't right for me. That's a sales rep I know I can trust."

> *"Prepare yourself in every way you can by increasing your knowledge and adding to your experience, so that you can make the most of opportunity when it occurs."*
>
> —MARIO ANDRETTI

[Know Your Product]

Once you've learned who a customer is and what his needs are, your goal is to match that customer with the product or service that suits him best. If your product doesn't qualify, you may have to walk away from that particular sale. But the only way you can know that for sure is to know your product inside and out.

"Knowledge is interchangeable with credibility," says Steve Sabol, vice president of sales of Green Mountain Coffee (wholesale coffee maker and distributor). "You can be the best listener, you can get past all the objections, you can be a great salesperson, but if you don't know your product, your proposed solution is going to be wrong for the customer, and it will come back to haunt you."

Green Mountain believes so strongly that knowledge is power that it has a "coffee college" program set up for new hires, and for potential and existing customers as well. The company brings these people to their facilities in Vermont so that their salespeople can "become engrossed in the coffee experience" and understand all the steps that are involved in manufacturing and producing a great cup of coffee.

"Some people forget that coffee is an agricultural product like corn or wheat, and that crops have good years and bad years. It's like wine in that sense," says Sabol. "It's really exciting for our new employees to come up here and immerse themselves in knowledge about coffee—what we call 'from bean to cup.' When you have solid grounding in what we do, along with how to become a business consultant for the customer, that's when you can make the best recommendations for your customers."

The sales reps at Green Mountain know their product inside out. Much of what they know, they may never share with their customers, but they know it nonetheless. And having the knowledge empowers them to pull information out when they are looking for solutions for customers. They're able to say, "You mentioned that these two factors are most important to you. Well, here's how our product can meet your needs in those areas. . . ." or "Here's how we can help you with this challenge and make it easier for you to . . ."

That is how you add value for your customers, and it's what makes you more valuable to your company as well.

But suppose your product is technically complex—for example, aeronautical equipment or supercomputers. In this case, you may need to go to the technicians in your company and ask them to explain exactly how your product works so that you're not just selling memorized features and benefits. The more you know about how your product works, the better you'll be able to understand how your product can solve your customers' problems.

That doesn't mean you have to be a walking encyclopedia. Learn as much as you can, and then make sure you know where to get information you may be lacking.

"The best salespeople in my company are not necessarily those with the most technical knowledge," says Chuck Parr of Ricoh. "The best salespeople are those who not only are diligent about educating themselves, but can go out and find other resources and use them effectively."

[Know Who You're Up Against]

Sometimes, the information customers want to know is how your product or service compares with the competition's.

This is often the case if you're selling a piece of equipment like a computer or a copier. Customers will ask how your brand compares to another one, what features your copier has, for instance, that another brand may not have, or what services you offer that another company doesn't. Sometimes, in order to be able to focus on your product's unique selling points, you have to know how they compare to and contrast with the competition's. When I sold copiers years ago, I had a printed sheet that compared my product to my competitors' so that prospects could see the differences in black and white. This comparison chart came from a non-biased source that conducted comparison studies, à la *Consumer Reports*. I could then line up my product against the other products the customer was considering, and compare it to the competition in terms of what that particular customer needed.

As a salesperson, you have to know what you're up against. Your product might be better than your competition's in some areas and not as good in others. What's most important is that you understand the client's needs. If your copier is faster than the competition's, for instance, and speed is of the essence for this client, then that's the feature of your copier you would emphasize. If your copier is slower than the competition's, you might emphasize that your company, because it is smaller, could provide better service without a lot of red tape—or any other feature that is important to the customer. This kind of product comparison not only reflects your product knowledge, but also shows the customer you've done your homework.

There are many ways to gather information about your competitors. You can use many of the same methods you use to research prospects' companies. You can look up their sites on the Internet. You can call the company and ask for brochures, product sheets, and catalogs that describe their products and services. You can study industry publications, business magazines, and newsletters. And you can talk to people in your company who have come from other industries and may have used your competitor's products—or even sold them.

Imitation (conscious or unconscious) is the trap of studying the competition. It's tempting to look not only at the competition's features and benefits, but also at how it's sold and marketed. Then you fall into "following the follower" and doing things because it's the way "everyone else does it." The best salespeople know enough about the competition to be able to answer customers' questions, and still have the single-minded focus to understand what makes their product stand out.

[Share *the* Wealth]

Knowledge is at its most powerful when it is being applied and when it is shared with others. And the best use of power is in giving something back to others around you—whether it is a way to assist them in solving their problems or as a helping hand in times of need.

That can be accomplished by looking toward others instead of ourselves. Turn your focus toward learning what is most important to someone else. Know what it is about your product or service that can help others achieve their goals. Learn about what makes your product or service unique among the rest. Then your success becomes dependent not on how many sales you can make, but on how many ways you can benefit others. As William H. Danforth, author of *I Dare You!*, once said, "Our most valuable possessions are those which can be shared without lessening; those which, when shared, multiply; our least valuable possessions are those which, when divided, are diminished."

Knowledge is a crucial asset to your ability to be successful—knowledge of your customers, of their needs, of your own product, of the competition. It all adds to tremendous confidence and competence when meeting customers face-to-face. Because when it comes down to the buying decision, customers feel that they're taking less of a risk when they're dealing with someone who exhibits that kind of knowledge. That's how trust is built, how relationships are formed, and how sales are made.

CHAPTER RECAP:
KNOWLEDGE IS POWER

[
*The more you know, the easier it is to come up
with solutions to your customers' problems.
That is what gives you added value,
what differentiates you from other sales reps.*
]

Know your customer.
- Any information you can get before a meeting can help you develop the right questions to ask. Learn the company's history and background, its products and services, and who its customers and competitors are.
- There are many resources to get this information:
  - Ask your contacts and mentors.
  - Use the Internet.
  - Study trade publications.
  - Ask to see company literature.

Think in questions.
- The most successful salespeople ask the best questions.
- Your goal is to determine whether the customer has a problem and what you can do to help.

Do your homework.
- Be thoroughly prepared for every sales presentation.
- Know your customer's business as well as your own.

Know your product.

- Use your knowledge to find solutions for your customers' problems.

Know who you're up against.

- Know how your brand compares to the competition's.
- Gather information about your competitors via the Internet, company literature, industry publications, and contacts who have used your competitor's products.
- Focus on how your product's strengths meet the customer's needs.

Share the wealth.

- Focus on learning what's most important to someone else.
- Your success depends not on how many sales you make, but on how many ways you can benefit others.

9

You Can't Fit *a* SQUARE Peg *into* *a* ROUND Hole

Some salespeople want so much to make a match, they'll try every which way possible to make their product fit a customer's needs. Sometimes it does, and sometimes it doesn't. There is only one way to find out, and that's by asking questions. Asking questions is essential to making sure your product is a good match with each prospective customer. In other

"It seems rather incongruous that in a society of super-sophisticated communication, we often suffer from a shortage of listeners."

—ERMA BOMBECK

words, you've got to determine that the person you're speaking to has a need for your product or service, has the money, and has the authority to buy. Otherwise, you end up wasting a lot of time—yours and theirs.

$$\left[\begin{array}{c} \text{Ask } \textit{the} \\ \textbf{Right Questions} \end{array}\right]$$

In the beginning of my sales career, I went back to a customer three times because I really didn't understand which product he wanted or needed. I had only one qualifying question: "Before we get started, if I could show you something that could benefit you and your business, do we have a basis for doing business today?" I fully expected the prospect to say yes. What could he possibly object to in that question? But I didn't really know where to go from there. I had no idea *what* would benefit that prospect, and I had no way to move the sale forward.

Experience taught me that I had to ask questions to pinpoint each customer's needs and desires. If I didn't qualify customers properly, not only did I waste a lot of time, but I also ultimately hurt my reputation, and my company's as well.

Qualifying is an art and a science that the best salespeople have learned to do well. It's all about pinpointing your customers' needs and what's important to them. It involves asking the right questions and listening carefully to the answers. Often it does not involve a lot of talking. Jeff Alpert, national sales manager for Green Mountain Coffee, feels that most salespeople talk too much because they think it puts them in control of the situation.

"In my experience," says Alpert, "you're in control when you're asking questions and listening. The other person is giving you all the ammunition you need to be successful in that sale. They'll give you every detail you need if you just ask the right questions and allow them to open up."

Alpert likes to begin by asking customers open-ended questions such as "What are your objectives?" and "What are the objectives of the organization?" Some other questions he recommends using are "What are your business drivers?" and "What are the things that are most challenging to you?"

"Regardless of the product you're selling," says Alpert, "open-ended questions enable you to make a contribution to the problems and concerns that are keeping your customers up at night. Those kinds of questions set the tone, not just for that day or that meeting, but for the entire relationship."

[The Four Big Qualifiers]

Qualifying is more than just understanding your customer's needs. It's understanding *your* needs as well. There are four main qualifying factors that a prospect should have. If one of these qualifying factors is missing, it doesn't make sense (for you or your prospect) to go on with the sale.

1. The decision-maker.

Has this ever happened to you? You work hard to perfect your presentation. You ask a prospect lots of questions to determine his needs, and realize that your product can provide several viable solutions for his problems. The prospect is obviously enthusiastic and shows real interest. You ask a closing question —and then the prospect says, "Sounds great to me. But I'll have to talk it over with my supervisor first."

Unfortunately, this is a scenario that happens all too often. Before you waste your precious time, it's imperative that you find out if the person you're speaking with has the authority to approve the purchase of your product or service. That's why selling from the top down is so important. You're working much more efficiently if you can get to the true decision-maker first. Here are three questions that will help you determine that you're talking to the right person:

- What is your role in the organization?

- Is there anyone else besides yourself who is involved with making this decision?

- Can you take me through the decision-making process that goes on when you're investing in this type of product or service?

2. Need.

If the customer doesn't need your product or service, there is no sale. It is possible to uncover a need the customer didn't know existed, but that need must then become obvious to both parties. Not only must you show the prospect that such a need exists, but you must also show how your particular product or service can meet that need. If there is nothing your product can do for a prospect, there is no motive for him to buy (and no reason for you to sell). Here are a few questions that will help you establish the customer's needs:

- What are your greatest challenges right now?

- What are your goals for the next year? For the next five years?

- If you could name three key things you're looking for from [fill in the name of your product or service], what would they be?

- What do you look for when choosing a new vendor? What are your expectations?

- What do you like about your present vendor in this area?

- If you could change something about your present vendor's product or service, what would it be?

3. Price.

Of course, every salesperson's dream is to sell her product or service for the highest price possible. But there are limits to what some prospects can spend. The better a customer understands the true value of your product or service, the more likely he is to pay a higher price for it.

However, based upon a prospect's needs, his budget estimate may not be realistic. He may be telling you that he wants to stay within a certain low price, but you know he won't be able to solve his problems using those parameters. It's as if a customer's need is to keep absolutely accurate time, yet he only wants to spend $10 for a watch. His limited budget won't allow him to meet that need. In that case, you will have to work harder to show him that he is being "penny wise and pound foolish" and that it will cost him more in the long run if he spends less up front and doesn't accomplish his goals. Here is the best question you can ask concerning price: "Can you give me an idea of the budget you have to invest in this service?"

4. Time frame.

Just when everything else is in place, when you think you've got the sale signed and sealed, you casually ask, "When would you like to have this delivered?" That's when the prospect says, "Oh, we've still got two years left on our current contract. But we'll definitely call you when the time is up." It's nice to have something to look forward to, but a lot can happen in two years. There may be some way to work the deal out so that the customer can get out of their lease, especially if the product they're using now is not meeting their current needs. If that's not the case, however, you don't want to waste your time (or theirs) when they're not ready to buy.

Or it could work the opposite way. The customer could answer, "We need your product by the day after tomorrow." In that case, be honest and say that you can't deliver by then. Once again, there may be a way to work it out. But if you know that it will take at least two weeks to deliver your product, you may have to walk away from this sale. In order to avoid both of these "untimely" situations, here are three questions you can ask concerning time frame:

- What is your time frame for this project?
- When are you looking to implement this program?
- When do you need this delivered?

The questions listed here are generic, of course, but they should give you some good qualifying information. You'll likely have other questions that are more specific to your particular industry.

[Three Major Mistakes]

Qualifying customers is one of the first rules of successful selling; however, it's something that takes practice to do well. Here are three major qualifying mistakes that salespeople make:

Mistake #1: *Not asking enough direct questions.* This is usually due to a lack of confidence. The reality is that customers usually appreciate your not beating around the bush. It means that you respect them and value their time, that you're not going to waste it. If you've been asking questions to understand their needs, they won't mind you asking direct questions (such as "What is your budget?").

Ann Hanford of Val-Pak thinks that many salespeople are afraid of asking direct questions, especially when it involves money. "I don't have a problem asking people if they have a budget," she says. "I want to know what it is so that I can help them get the most bang for their bucks. If they don't have the budget I think they need, we may have to regroup. But if I don't ask, I have no way of knowing how I can help them."

It helps to ask yourself why you are afraid of asking a direct question. Is it because the more direct the question, the greater the possibility of a direct rejection? Or is it because you don't want to find out if a prospect is not qualified, and have to end the sale right there?

You need only be afraid of rejection if this one sale is so important to you that you can't afford to lose it. If you have enough other irons in the fire, the worst the prospect can say is no. When you have spent the time to qualify a prospect, and you know that there is a match between your product and his needs, you have earned the right to ask a question like "What do we need to do to move this forward?"

Mistake #2: *Assuming one person can give you all the answers.*
Besides asking if there is anyone else who is involved in making

the decision, ask if there is anyone else who can give you input about the needs of the company. There may be people in other positions or departments who have a slightly different take on any one of the four main qualifying factors. This is especially important if you're dealing with a complex product or service and a long sales cycle. When you combine the information you get from three or four people in the organization, you can make a strong presentation that covers a variety of contingencies.

Mistake #3: *Getting too excited before the dotted line is signed.* Things may seem to be going well. You're confident that the deal is moving toward the close, and you're just waiting for the paperwork to come through. Unfortunately, that's when many salespeople slack off because they think they've got a done deal. But this is the time when your efforts should be redoubled. Don't disappear when the customer is ready to sign. They may need some additional hand-holding and final reassurances that they are getting the value they originally perceived.

[Silence Is Golden]

Those three mistakes can be costly, but they're easily rectified. There is one more mistake, however, that is perhaps the most common one that salespeople make, and one that can be more difficult to remedy.

Salespeople talk too much.

This chapter has been about understanding the needs and wants of the customer. How is it possible to discover what those wants and needs are if you're doing all the talking? Imagine that you were an investigator, trying to determine someone's motives for taking a particular action. Would you go in and start rattling off theories until you came upon one that made sense? Of course not. You could go on forever without hitting on the one true reason. So how does an investigator uncover the suspect's true motive? By asking the right questions and getting the suspect to reveal his innermost secrets.

The same concept applies to sales. If you go in to see a prospect and start spouting off reasons you *think* he might want or need your product, you could go on forever without hitting on his one true need. If you're truly interested in qualifying prospects, you will ask questions, stop talking, and listen.

A while back, I spoke with Bill Crosby, general manager of dispenser services for Green Mountain Coffee, who described one of the most interesting sales calls he ever went on. He and a sales rep were calling on a prospect who bought coffee for sixty to seventy college campuses, and both were very excited about the possibility of getting this business.

"We sat down in this buyer's office," says Crosby, "and the first thing the rep said was 'I have no idea whether I can help you with this program or not. I've had tremendous success with similar customers, but until I learn more about your situation, there's no way for me to know whether this is a good fit or not.'

"This took the purchasing agent aback. He was used to reps coming in and saying, 'I know I can sell this product, and I know you need to buy it.' Then they'd go straight into their product patter. But the Green Mountain rep started right off by asking to learn about this man's company to see if his product was compatible with the prospect's business vision. The buyer loved it. We ended up staying for an hour and a half when we'd been scheduled for half an hour. And we ended up getting a large piece of business."

Early in my sales career, when I had few sales skills, I relied on my enthusiasm and persistence to carry me past my lack of technique. But after a while, I realized that my enthusiasm, while a positive asset in many ways, was getting in my way. I would get so excited, I wasn't listening; I was so anxious to tell "my side of the story" that I kept interrupting my prospects. At one point, my sales manager told me to write the word *listen* on top of my notepad before I started to ask any questions. He told me that I should be listening at least 70 percent of the time during a sales call.

That piece of advice has stayed with me through the years, and it has served me well. I have learned to respect my customers' time as well as my own. And I have learned that it's more important for me to understand my customers than to try to "convince" them into a sale.

Customers want somebody to listen to them, but most

salespeople tend to talk right through them. They're so busy thinking about what their next question should be, they don't hear what the customer is saying. If somebody wants to talk to you about what a rotten weekend they had or about the new dog they just bought, take ten extra minutes and just listen. That's the start of your relationship.

Remember the old sales cliché that goes, "Nobody ever listened themselves out of a sale." But some salespeople have *talked* themselves out of a sale by bringing up factors that the prospect had perhaps not even considered. For instance, a salesperson can get very excited about a particular feature and start talking it up: "This camera focuses automatically, but it has this great option that allows you to manually change the f-stops and focus it yourself." That may be a wonderful option, but not what this amateur photographer is interested in. In fact, instead of being a benefit to this prospect, it may be a detraction. Although it's tempting to just go through an entire presentation and hope that some of your points hit home, what happens instead is that the prospect hears more than is necessary and can't focus on the benefits that most suit his needs.

The truth is that people don't retain an overload of information. If you include too many facts and details, their minds will begin to wander. Some studies have shown that the average person's attention span is only about eight seconds! So you're better off concentrating on the two or three main points that are most important to your prospect.

[The Energy *of* Listening]

I've heard sales reps say, "I'm willing to listen, but sometimes it's hard to get customers talking." Remember that most people love to talk. Most of all, they love to talk about themselves, and they love to talk about the things that interest them. You can sometimes get reluctant talkers started by asking questions like "How long have you been in this business?" and "What is the thing you like most about this job? This company?"

By asking sincere questions and patiently waiting for a response before moving on to the next question, you show concern for the customer. If you skip through the questions and don't wait for a sound answer, you demonstrate insincerity. It shows you don't really care about the answers—you're just asking questions for effect. This will give the customer an adverse impression—it will anger him because you're wasting his time and you're trying to con him by acting as if you care.

On the other hand, you show people how much you care by focusing on ways to make them feel important. Often, just giving customers your undivided attention will make them feel important. Concentrate on discovering what concerns them most at that moment, and then let them know you understand those concerns and that you'll do your best to help alleviate them.

You can sometimes get customers talking by asking such

open-ended questions as "Can you expand on that?," "Tell me more about that . . . ," "Can you go into detail about . . . ," or "What do you mean?"

Another technique is called "parroting." This is a more subtle way of getting people to expand their thoughts. A conversation might go:

Customer: "Our biggest concern right now is getting into new markets."

Rep: "New markets?"

Customer: "Yes. We're going into two new areas, one where we've never had a rep before, and one where we've had problems in the past."

Rep: "Problems in the past?"

Customer: "When we went out there last time . . ."

Of course, you don't use this technique after every sentence, but it is a signal to the customer that you're really listening to what he's saying and that you're interested in knowing more. The more you know, the more value you can add to your package.

Also, watch your customer's body language. If the customer is looking directly at you, is leaning in toward you, and is using animated gestures, he's showing signs of interest. If he's leaning back and won't look you in the eye, you might be wise to move on to another area. But bear in mind that body language is not always easy to read. A person sitting with crossed legs and arms may be chilly, not unfriendly.

Because listening is so intangible, it's necessary to acknowledge that you're listening, to let your prospect know that you are paying attention.

Be sure you make regular eye contact with the prospect, nod your head, and add a verbal acknowledgment ("Is that so?" or "That's interesting") every once in a while.

It's also wise to take notes. Someone once said, "A short pencil is better than a long memory." Note-taking not only helps you remember what went on at your meeting, but also makes the prospect feel important. Every once in a while, reiterate what the prospect has told you.

> *"A good listener is not only popular everywhere, but after a while he knows something."*
>
> —WILSON MIZNER

For instance, after a prospect or customer has made an important point, you could say, "Let me be sure I've got this straight. You're saying that if we do this, that would be important to you?" Rephrase the prospect's comments to guarantee you're on the same wavelength.

Reinforce the fact that you've been listening by sending the prospect a follow-up letter after the meeting, highlighting the key points that were covered. Since most sales are lost due to a lack of communication, this is another way to ensure that you and your customer understand each other.

Active listening requires energy and effort in order to absorb everything that is being said. You've got to put your own agenda aside for a while and focus on your customer's. Use all of the listening skills you have to probe for more information than a customer may initially be willing to give. If your skills need some work, there are some things you can do to improve them.

- ❑ **Paint mind pictures.** We all do it. We're paying attention, we're listening, we're hearing every word, and then . . . we're not. We're drifting. A customer is talking to you about his manufacturing plant and his newly revised and automated delivery system, and suddenly you're thinking, "If I can get out of here in half an hour, I can get to the gym before seven. What should I have for dinner? I've got to call Susan. . . ." Then out of nowhere, you suddenly hear, "What do you think about that?" That's when you know you're in trouble.

  To help you stay focused when people are talking about things that may not be of the greatest interest to you, paint mind pictures of what they are saying. Create a mental image and try to make it as complete as possible. If parts of the picture are missing, ask questions until you can fill them in.

- ❑ **Concentrate.** Listening is not a gift; it's a skill that takes work. No matter how easy it looks, there is effort involved. Anyone can hear, but not everyone can listen effectively. Most people only half-listen; they tend to make assumptions about what the prospect really means and then jump to conclusions about what he really needs. When you truly concentrate, however, you make a commitment to focus on the customer and to pay attention to exactly what he's saying.

❑ **Remember past successes**. Think about sales calls and meetings that worked for you before. For me, those meetings were the ones where I talked the least and got the prospects most involved. Then, when it came my time to speak, my presentation was solid and tied in to the customer's needs.

Qualifying is all about understanding—understanding your customers' needs, making sure that your product or service can be of benefit so that it makes sense to move forward with the sale. The days of pushing products just to make commissions are over. It will cost you sales when customers find out they've gotten something they really don't want and can't use. What is critical is seeing the world from your customers' perspective. Customers want a salesperson who is not only an expert on what he sells, but also an expert on matching his product or service with their goals and challenges.

CHAPTER RECAP:
YOU CAN'T FIT *a* SQUARE PEG *into a* ROUND HOLE

[
Make sure that each prospect has a need for your product or service, can pay the price, and has the authority to buy. Otherwise, you waste your time—and theirs.
]

Three big mistakes salespeople make when qualifying:
1. Not asking enough questions.
2. Assuming one person can give you all the answers.
3. Getting too excited before the dotted line is signed.

Silence is golden.
- Listen more than you talk.
- Do not look for reasons you think the prospect might want or need your product; let the prospect state his or her needs.

The energy of listening.
- Active listening requires energy and effort.
- Ask questions to get reluctant talkers started.
- Don't just ask questions—listen carefully to the answers.
- Ask open-ended questions.
- Use "parroting" to get people to expand their thoughts.

- Watch your customers' body language.
- Make regular eye contact.
- Reinforce the fact that you've been listening by sending follow-up letters.
- Improve your listening skills by:
  - Painting mind pictures.
  - Concentrating.
  - Remembering past success.

10 Don't Sell *the* Steak, Sell *the* SIZZLE

The phrase "Don't sell the steak, sell the sizzle" first appeared in 1936, when, according to Elmer Wheeler, it was deemed to be "principle number one of salesmanship."

"It is the sizzle that sells the steak and not the cow, although the cow is, of course, mighty important," he said.

When you've qualified your prospects, when you've listened to their needs and special problems, it's your turn to sell the

> *"It usually takes more than three weeks to prepare a good impromptu speech."*
>
> —MARK TWAIN

sizzle. This is when you get to make your presentation—to tell customers about your product or service, but, more importantly, about what your product or service can do for them. Selling the sizzle means making it possible for a prospect to smell that steak cooking, hear the fat dripping into the fire, see the juices running down into the plate, and taste that smoky barbecue flavor even when there's nothing at all in front of him except you. You're selling the pleasure and satisfaction that steak will bring.

Today, selling the sizzle goes even beyond its original concept. Because today, selling the sizzle means selling more than features and benefits; it means helping the prospect solve problems. Your job is to be a consultant to your customer's business, to be a specialist in your particular field so that, like a doctor, you can diagnose your customer's problem and figure out how to cure it. Your presentation should be a prescription for what ails the company, and your product or service, taken as directed, should be the cure. It will help the company feel better, do more, and be healthier than ever.

The purpose of your presentation is to explain your diagnosis and demonstrate its cure.

[Un-Canny Presentations]

Presentations come in many different packages—they range from a formal speech to a casual conversation. No matter what format it takes, the worst way a presentation can come is in a can. That's why it's so difficult for most telemarketers to make a sale. When you're simply reading from a script, and it's the same script for everyone, it's not easy to convince a prospect that you care anything about her.

It may be possible to sell using a canned spiel. It's been done. Most of the time, however, this kind of super-rehearsed presentation results in buyer's remorse, returns, and complaints. Customers may be swayed enough to buy, but they soon realize that what they bought isn't fulfilling any of their needs.

Your goal is to present an idea, a concept, a product or service you feel would benefit your particular customers. It's up to you to be sure they understand how your product relates to their needs. You have to be able to demonstrate this connection simply and clearly for your prospect. The stronger the connection, the more likely the sale. That means you have to be sure you know your audience and thoroughly understand what's important to them.

"Knowing your audience is as important as what you are presenting," says Betty Jagoda Murphy of Creative Products Resource, Inc., an organization that gets other companies to invest in new products and inventions.

"If we're presenting to a consumer products company, for example, we should be familiar with the products they sell, how those products are doing in the marketplace, and what their customers like about those products. That way, we can position our new product to fit into their current line. We want to make them feel comfortable that what we are selling will increase their value."

Murphy explains that the companies she's presenting to have to understand clearly the value her new product will bring to their own business. They want to know that investing in her product will give them a leg up over the competition. They also want to know that her product will get their shareholders excited, so her presentations have to demonstrate vividly how what she is selling will improve the investor's business.

"Last year, we came up with a two-action dishwashing product," says Murphy. "So we researched all the companies that deal in this type of product. Then we chose to present the product to the company that would have the most to lose if someone else came out with that product. We made up boxes of our dishwashing powder using that company's brand names to make it easier for them to 'see' our product in their line.

"Their original objection was that selling one product that performed two functions would cannibalize two of their current products. Our presentation, however, showed how this product would, in fact, increase their sales because it would attract a whole new group of consumers away from their competitors' products. We were able to turn them around from worrying about their current business to believing they could attract brand-new users."

Every presentation you make should be custom-designed to fit that customer's needs. A few years ago, I approached three different radio syndicators about the prospect of taking on my talk show about achievement, "Diamond in the Rough." Before I started describing the program, I asked each of them this question: "What are the three most important things you're looking for when investing in a new radio program?"

The first syndicator listed "entertainment value, quality content, and a program that can attract advertisers." The second man said, "a host who is easy to get along with, who can book high-profile guests, and who can attract advertisers." The third man replied that the three most important things to him were "making money, making money, and making money."

Three different customers, three different answers. Naturally, I focused my presentation differently to each man, stressing the benefits that best met each one's criteria for investing in a new show. When you take the time to focus on each customer's special needs, you've earned the right to make your presentation. If you make the same pitch to everyone, you'll surely miss the boat—and the sale.

Steve Miller is vice president of sales for Great-West Life Insurance. He says that many salespeople, especially new reps, are taught canned presentation skills by their organizations. They think that selling is going out and regurgitating this presentation, and that the buyer will listen and say, "That's wonderful. I'll take it." Naturally, the salesperson gets discouraged when prospects don't respond to this preplanned, impersonal sales approach.

But there are other reasons salespeople don't ask enough questions. "Many times, they're afraid to ask," says Miller, "because they're afraid they'll get answers they can't deal with on their feet. So they do their canned presentation and walk away thinking, 'Gee, that went really well,' even though they have no clue about what the buyer is thinking. Meanwhile, they've missed all the critical components that go into making a sale."

What they miss, according to Miller, is the opportunity to "read the buyer." Is the prospect absorbing the information that you're giving him? Does it make sense to him? Is he turned on by it, or is he ambivalent? You have to listen to the prospect's answers, watch his facial expressions, and measure to what degree he participates in your presentation.

"Then you have to learn to act on those signals, and that's something that comes with experience. After you're done with the sales call, you have to have an honest postmortem. Did you really observe the buyer? Did you ask questions at the beginning, middle, and end of the call that could give you a clear indication of what the buyer was feeling about doing business with you?"

If you can answer these questions honestly and positively, then you have established a relationship with this buyer and greatly improved your chances of making the sale.

[Deliver *with* Style]

A good presentation is an entertaining, engaging interchange between the person who is making the presentation and the audience. That doesn't mean that you have to be a performer or a magician or a professional comedian. It doesn't mean your presentation has to be filled with bells, whistles, and special effects. But you do want your presentation to be vivid, convincing, and memorable.

The best way to do that is to put passion into your presentation. Passion can lift your spirits and give you the energy you need to get others as excited about your presentation as you are. Passion comes naturally when you truly believe in what you're selling, when you are certain beyond a doubt that your product or service has strong benefits for your prospects and customers.

Passion comes through when you talk about more than just facts. Use stories to illustrate your points. You can talk about how other customers with similar needs used your product or service to solve their problems. If you have a testimonial from a customer to back up what you're saying, incorporate it into your presentation.

Another way to keep your audience involved throughout your presentation is to use vivid language that conjures up mental pictures that enable your prospects to imagine themselves using your product or service. You want to communicate that you're saving them time, saving them effort, increasing their profits— whatever the appropriate benefit. "The best thing about our product is that service is built in every thirty days. You don't even have to think about making a service call. It's automatic!" Express anything that might be a problem or challenge with their present equipment that your product or service will eliminate.

The key to developing a solid presentation style is to recognize your strengths and build on them. If you're a born raconteur, incorporate more stories into the presentation. If you're not, use fewer stories. Strong delivery comes with practice and experience. Be yourself, be enthusiastic, and be real. That's all your customers want and expect.

[What Is *a* Picture Worth?]

Many times, a picture really is worth a thousand words. Visual aids can portray—vividly and instantly—things that would take volumes to explain verbally. They save time, create interest, add variety, and help your audience remember your main points.

However, visual aids also have a dark side. They take a great deal of time and thought—and sometimes money—to create; they can take attention away from what you're saying; and if anything goes wrong, they can be a catastrophe.

A visual aid can be any sort of prop you use to support your ideas and concepts, including charts, graphs, photographs, slides, and handouts. A good visual aid can make your presentation more effective, but remember that it is an aid, and not a replacement for strong content.

When I first started out in sales, I used to think that more was better. I came equipped with dozens of articles and testimonials and charts and leave-behinds. Slowly, I began to realize that a few really strong pieces were much more effective.

However, because I, like Steve Miller, prefer to overprepare, I sometimes bring lots of materials with me to meetings, especially if the meeting is very important. Recently, I had a hard-won appointment with a major television executive. I thought of everything he might like to see about me. So I stuffed my briefcase with books and tapes, articles I had written, and articles that had been written about me. I was ready to pull any rabbit out of that hat.

When the executive asked me a question about my background and experience, I started to reach into my case to pull out some materials. But he looked at me and said, "I don't need to see any of that. Let's just talk." That was fine with me, and that's what happened. Had I been relying on my materials to speak for me, however, I would have been up a creek.

There are other times I go to sales calls with nothing but a pad and pen in hand. These are times when it is more important for me to find out about the customer and the company. Sometimes, I have sent them my materials beforehand; sometimes, I will send them after the meeting, when I have determined that our two companies could benefit each other. What you bring, and how much you bring, depends on the individual situation.

There are some industries where sales reps are taught to rely on visual aids. Many sales reps in the pharmaceuticals industry, for example, are given detail sheets (which contain facts and findings about particular drugs) and are told that they must share these with the doctors they see. The problem is that the doctors see dozens of these sheets each week from every sales-person who stops by their offices. After a while, the sheets lose their impact.

Sometimes, it's better to forget about the detail sheet and do something that makes you stand out from the crowd. I once rode along with a sales rep from Schering Diabetes. He stopped off before going in to see one doctor and bought lunch for the whole office. Instead of the usual ten minutes most sales reps get to spend with a doctor (if they're lucky), he spent ten minutes just listening to the doctor tell him about a ski trip he'd recently taken with his son. Then the rep got to spend the rest of the lunchtime asking the doctor questions about how his patients were doing on Schering products.

He also asked the doctor a very effective question. He said, "Doctor, if you were me and you were speaking to other doctors about this product, how would you present it to them?" The doctor spoke to him for several minutes about the success he has had with this product, and how he uses it in his practice. Then, when we went to the next doctor, the sales rep used the first doctor's testimonial during his presentation. This information now had the credibility of a doctor's opinion behind it. The sales rep still had his detail sheets to leave with the doctor for reference, but he used much more creative methods to make the sale.

Visual aids can be effective reminders to leave with people after you've gone. But remember that customers and prospects are buying you as well as your product. If that were not true, salespeople would be obsolete and companies could just send their information out alone and expect a prospect to buy.

Getting Over *the* Fear Factor

Studies have shown that the greatest fear for most people is not the fear of death (number two on the list), but the fear of speaking in public. That means we would rather be in the casket at a funeral than giving the eulogy! As writer Roscoe Drummond once said, "The mind is a wonderful thing—it starts working the minute you're born and never stops until you get up to speak in public."

In selling, we're confronted with fear every day—fear of cold calls, fear of rejection, fear of asking for the business, fear of making presentations, and fear of not measuring up to other people's expectations (not to mention our own). Fear can send unwelcome thoughts roaring through your brain: "What if I'm asked a question I can't answer?" "What if my sales manager sees me fall flat on my face?" "What if I'm so boring they all fall asleep?" These questions run rampant, even though most of the time you say to yourself after the presentation, "That wasn't so bad after all." Fear makes your imagination work overtime, and it is what blocks people from achieving their potential in sales more than any other barrier.

But once you understand how your imagination can distort reality, you can focus on your preparation and on finding out the customer's needs, rather than watching yourself perform.

Almost all salespeople experience a certain amount of anxiety before making a presentation. The best cure for this is experience. The more presentations you make, the better they will be. It's the only way to eliminate the fear that most salespeople—especially those just starting out—experience before making a presentation.

Remember that fear can also be a good thing. It can be used to fire you up and get your adrenaline pumping. It can help you focus your energies on producing positive results. The fear of failure often forces us to be thoroughly prepared to reduce the possibility of mistakes and missteps. And always keep in mind these words of wisdom from Mark Twain: "Fear came knocking at the door, faith answered and no one was there."

> *"The only thing we have to fear is fear itself."*
> —*FRANKLIN DELANO ROOSEVELT*

[Eleven Steps *to a* Successful Presentation]

Understanding the needs of your audience is the key element to a successful presentation. If you are tuned in to your audience, even a poorly delivered presentation can be well received; if you're not, even a polished one can fall flat.

However, your goal is always to deliver the best presentation possible. Here are eleven steps you can take to make that happen.

1. Determine your purpose.

Of course, your ultimate goal is to make a sale, but that is not necessarily the reason for your presentation. If you're selling vending machines, for instance, the goal may be to have the prospect agree to install a machine in his office for a week to get feedback from his employees. If you're dealing with a long and complicated sales cycle, the purpose of your meeting may be to secure a second appointment to meet with other executive committee members. Or the purpose may be for the prospect to supply you with the information you need to submit a formal proposal. It's important that you determine your purpose before you get to the meeting, and stay focused on it until you accomplish your goal.

2. *Visualize a successful outcome.*

Run through the entire process in your mind. Reiterate the most important points you want to make. Go over your research and the benefits you think will be most important to this prospect. Picture yourself confident, knowledgeable, articulate, and able to handle whatever comes your way.

I've interviewed hundreds of successful people, and one of the strongest traits they had in common was the ability to see themselves as successful before they ever reached their goals.

3. *Find out how much time you will have.*

The ideal sales situation is when you're scheduled for a half-hour meeting with a prospect or customer that stretches into an hour or longer. That means the customer is truly interested in what you have to say. Unfortunately, there are times when, interested or not, prospects have other obligations. You could find yourself in the middle of what you've planned to be an hour-long presentation when your client says, "I'm sorry, but I've got to go now!" Your best bet is to ask at the beginning of the call how much time has been set aside. Then you must be flexible enough to change your presentation to fit the time frame. It's also important that you honor an agreed-upon time frame. If a prospect says he only has twenty minutes to spare, that's all the time you should take. If the prospect is interested in hearing more, he will either extend your meeting or ask you to come back at another time.

4. Build rapport.

You probably won't have a lot of time for small talk, but a short time spent getting to know someone is never wasted. If you have time before your appointment, ask the prospect's assistant or secretary if he or she can give you any information about the prospect that might be useful, as I did before the meeting described in chapter 2, when the assistant of the man I was meeting told me her boss was an avid Mets fan and I was able to incorporate that into my presentation. Try to find areas of interest you and the prospect can chat about briefly. Look around the office and see if there is any common ground to give the conversation a smooth start.

5. Qualify.

Use the questioning techniques in the previous chapter to determine the customer's needs and uncover the four main qualifying factors. Although you have probably qualified the prospect before the meeting, you can expand on this during the presentation and get any additional information you might need. During this needs analysis stage, you will be doing more listening than talking. You should also be taking notes so that the rest of your presentation will address any concerns the customer has expressed.

6. Focus on key points.

Decide on at least three crucial points you want to make, hot buttons that will get the buyer excited. Then be prepared to add or subtract from these points as you get more information from your qualifying questions.

"I go into every presentation overprepared," says Steve Miller of Great-West Life Insurance. "I can always back off. Oftentimes I come out of a presentation not using eighty percent of what I went in with. But I'd much rather be in that position. I see too many salespeople go in on the fly, underprepared, and it's a complete waste of time."

Present your ideas from your prospect's perspective. People buy for their reasons, not yours. When you're tuned in to a prospect or customer, you understand what's most important to him. It is empathy—the ability to understand what others are feeling—that gives a successful salesperson the competitive edge.

7. Differentiate yourself.

Always keep in mind a list of three things that make you, your company, and your product or service unique. Prospects want to know what you can bring to the table that no one else can. Make sure they know how your unique strengths will be of benefit to them and try to provide practical solutions to their problems.

8. Keep your audience involved.

Just because it's your turn to speak doesn't mean you need to turn a presentation into a lecture. You want to get your prospects emotionally involved in the sale. Keep asking for their feedback. Every few minutes, ask questions to ascertain whether or not you're on the right track. You can also use trial closing questions to be sure you're on target; for example, "Based upon what we've talked about so far, is this of interest to you?"

9. Summarize.

Go back over the key points you've made and the key concerns the prospect has raised. This allows you to make sure you're communicating well and that you have interpreted your prospect's needs correctly. Show the prospect that you've listened to what's important to him, and connect your product to those needs. If you haven't done these things, the prospect can now point you back in the right direction. Just before you close, you can ask, "Is there anything else I haven't covered or any questions I haven't answered?"

10. Close.

Keep your purpose in mind, and close for the next step. That could be getting more information ("Is there someone I can speak to in the shipping department so that I can get a better idea of your needs in that area?"), securing a demonstration ("Can we set up an appointment for next Tuesday so that I can come back and show you exactly how my product will meet your needs?"), or asking for the order ("Why don't we go ahead with this today?").

11. Follow through.

This one is simple—don't make promises you can't keep. I constantly am amazed when I interview my customers' customers and they tell me about salespeople who don't follow through on their promises. As Peter Johnson, vice president of Boston Bean, puts it, "People come in here and put on a nice big dog and pony show. Then they say, 'I'll get back to you next week with answers to your questions or with some ideas for a sales contest that we could run.' But they don't call me back or they don't show up for their appointment. It's a total negative, and something I don't understand. And I certainly won't do business with them or their company again."

Strong follow-through is what keeps customers loyal, and the best salespeople make it a part of their sales philosophy.

Four Things NOT *to* Do When Making *a* Presentation

A mediocre presentation can lose the sale for even the greatest product or service. Keeping that in mind, here are the five most important things not to do when making a presentation.

1. Don't make your presentation the same for everyone.

No two customers are the same, so no two presentations should be the same. The best presentation is the one that is focused on why this particular customer should buy this particular product. In order to do that, present your ideas from the customer's perspective, and make the connections between product and benefits clear.

2. Don't wing it.

Don't go into your meeting blind. Do your research before you get there so that you are ready with ideas of what the customer's challenges might be and how your product might be able to help solve their problems.

3. Don't do all the talking.

The purpose of your presentation is to make it easy for your customer to buy. Customers want to buy when you are focused on their real needs; by asking questions, you get customers to reveal their problems and challenges. Then you can concentrate on presenting solutions that make sense for them and their business.

4. Don't be disorganized.

When your ideas are organized, you can focus on your message. You want to be sure your audience can follow your train of thought from beginning to end. There are four steps you can take to keep your presentation running smoothly, and they are an old sales cliché that says, "Tell them what you're going to tell them; tell them; test them; and tell them what you told them."

❑ **Tell them what you're going to tell them.** Let them know what to expect in the presentation and why your solution makes sense. For instance, you might say, "I'm now going to take you through our new product line and demonstrate exactly how it will help you decrease production time." Get them excited about what they're about to hear.

❑ **Tell them.** Go through your presentation following the outline you just proposed.

❑ **Test them.** Keep your prospects involved. Ask questions that will let you know if the presentation is hitting home and addressing their criteria. Ask, "Is that important to you?" or "Do you see how this could help eliminate the service problem you had in the past?"

❑ **Tell them what you told them.** Summarize your ideas and the most important benefits you covered in your presentation. Leave them with a succinct summary of the points that are most important to them.

Franklin Delano Roosevelt may have had the best advice ever for anyone giving a presentation: "Be brief. Be sincere. Be seated." Speak from the heart and get your message across. Then sit down.

CHAPTER RECAP:
DON'T SELL *the* STEAK, SELL *the* SIZZLE

[
*Selling the sizzle means selling
more than features and benefits.
It means helping prospects solve problems.*
]

Un-canny presentations.

- You need to be able to demonstrate clearly the connection between your product and the customer's needs.
- You need to thoroughly understand your audience.
- Every presentation should be custom-designed according to each customer's needs.

Deliver with style.

- A good presentation is vivid, convincing, and memorable.
- Put passion into your presentations.
- Use stories to illustrate your points.
- Use vivid language.
- Build on your strengths.

What is a picture worth?

- Use visual aids, but use them carefully.
- Be prepared in case something goes wrong with the visual aids you'd planned to use.

Getting over the fear factor.
- Understand that your imagination can distort reality.
- Focus on your preparation and on finding out the customer's needs, rather than watching yourself perform.
- Use fear to get your adrenaline pumping.

Eleven steps to a successful presentation.
1. Determine your purpose.
2. Visualize a successful outcome.
3. Find out how much time you will have.
4. Build rapport.
5. Qualify.
6. Focus on key points.
7. Differentiate yourself.
8. Keep your prospects involved.
9. Summarize.
10. Close.
11. Follow through.

Four things not to do when making a presentation. Don't:
1. Make your presentation the same for everyone.
2. Wing it.
3. Do all the talking.
4. Be disorganized.

Be brief, be sincere, be seated.

11 You Get What You Pay For

"You get what you pay for" is a sales cliché that most salespeople misinterpret. They think it means that if you pay a high price for something, you'll get good quality and service—and if you don't, you won't. Successful salespeople interpret this cliché differently. To them, it means that when you buy something from them, no matter what you pay for it, you'll get your money's worth. In fact, you'll get more.

High achievers are not content merely to do what everyone

> *"What we obtain too cheap, we esteem too lightly; it is the dearness only that gives everything value."*
>
> —THOMAS PAINE

else is doing. They go beyond. They constantly are asking themselves, "What else can I offer?"

Selling is tough today, and if adding value for your customers is not a high priority for you, you will simply not make it to the top of this profession. Things are changing too rapidly to let yourself become complacent. Competitors' prices drop in an instant. Every time you turn around, there is another product out on the market that is exactly like yours. Where, then, does your value lie?

It lies within you. You must be the final deciding factor that makes a prospect choose your product over all the others.

Every customer wants to know what he is getting for his money. And every customer wants to pay the lowest price possible. Most customers—and salespeople—get hung up on dealing with issues of price, and forget about the issue of value. That's because value is much more difficult to sell and more difficult to measure. To value something means to consider its worth, excellence, usefulness, or importance. Therefore, value is relative to the needs of the individual, whereas a price is a price is a price. The most successful salespeople constantly sell value; the least successful rely on price.

"The first thing everybody talks about is price," says Ben Forester, president of Rex Lumber Company in Englishtown, New Jersey. "Everybody understands that six dollars is more than five dollars. You have to help customers understand why they should pay the six dollars. They have to know, for instance, that we have a huge inventory, that we can deliver whenever they need it. That comes at a cost, but in the long run, the fact that we can deliver the lumber quickly and all at once is more valuable than the dollars. If you can get it for less, but you can't get it when you need it, what good is it?

"I think, overall, price is about fourth on the list of reasons to buy. Number one is the confidence you have in the person you're dealing with. Second is service, and third is reliability. It's your track record that builds a customer's confidence in a vendor. You've got to be able to say, 'Try us, and we'll prove that we will consistently do what no one else will.'"

Many salespeople tell me they've lost sales to the competition, only to find that the customer came back to them because they did not get what they needed. They went with the competition because the price was lower, but ended up returning to their original vendor to get the service they missed. As a salesperson, your job is to help customers see the big picture, that there is more involved than just the cost of the item.

"For the salesperson, the big task in selling value is helping the customer understand the other elements besides price," says Robert Shipley of Unilever. "Take Suave hair care, for instance. Suave certainly has a very good price, and it works as well as the more expensive brands, but equally important is that it's relevant to the customer. It has everything the consumer looks for in hair care. It might be color protection, or extra body, or moisturizing.

"The value in Suave comes from being relevant to the consumer, delivering the performance they expect, and having the price that surprises them. But if you just focus on price, ultimately no one wins. You start to take the quality out."

Customers always look for a good bargain; it's human nature. But they're smart enough to know that price isn't the whole story—even if they sometimes need to be reminded of that fact. I once heard about a hair salon in a fairly well-to-do neighborhood that charged only $10 for haircuts. One slow month, as a special promotion, they put out a big sign advertising haircuts for $6. Up the road, there was a high-end salon that started losing business to customers who were going in for the cheap cut. They soon remedied the situation by putting up their own sign: WE FIX $6 HAIRCUTS.

[Ways *to* Add Value]

When I do seminars, I try my best to give a presentation unlike any my audience has participated in before. I don't just do a needs analysis with the people who hire. I spend many hours on the phone with their salespeople, and also with their customers. I interview their customers on tape and play back some of the comments during the seminar. These customers tell the salespeople what they're doing right, and what they're not doing that the customers would appreciate. This is something different that not too many other people do, and it adds value to my seminar.

There are many different kinds of value that can help sell your product. There is, for instance, emotional value.

This is the type of value that Christopher Radko offers. Radko manufactures and sells exquisite (and expensive) hand-made Christmas ornaments. Each ornament takes seven days to make by specialized craftspeople. There is one woman who is known as the "eyelash lady," for example, and she paints on all the eyelashes. Another painter works only on hands, and another one works on belts and boots, and so on. The execution of detail is very precise. The workmanship is so fine that the high price of his ornaments is easily justified.

However, it's not only craftsmanship that Radko is selling. "There's the emotional value that we offer," says Radko. "For many people, Christmas ornaments are a bridge to creating memories or remembering previous holidays with friends and family. So our salespeople are in the business of promoting the heart of Christmas.

"Our job is to connect people to each other, one ornament at a time. If sales reps understand that, if that resonates within their being and they're passionate about that, they can go forth and sell that connection, each in his or her own creative way."

That creativity often comes out in how the sales representatives work with the store owners selling Radko's ornaments. They don't just deliver the ornaments in boxes and stack them on shelves; they create a unique selling environment.

They create a mini-theater of ornaments to draw customers in, which helps sell everything else in the store along with Radko's Christmas decorations. So they've created added value for the store owner and for the end consumer as well.

Radko's reps continue that added-value selling with community involvement. "During breast cancer week, we might have a doctor from the local hospital come in to the store to talk to customers, or during the holiday season, we might sponsor the high school choir to come in and sing," says Radko. "We help retailers stay connected to the community. Then they never have to worry about being replaced by the Internet. Every time a rep holds a special event at a store, it's another chance for interaction with the collectors and with the store owners. It's a successful tool for a good sell-through, and a great way to add value."

The concept of adding value applies no matter what you sell. Every time you go into an organization and ask questions about the company's needs and goals, you have another opportunity to look for ways you can support their vision. That might mean recommending another vendor who can help them in an area outside your expertise. Highly successful salespeople have a network of names and contacts in a variety of industries they can recommend as resources for their prospects and customers.

An added-value approach to selling puts you in a whole new light for your customers. You become one of their company's assets, one that they will not trade in easily for another vendor.

The Value *of the* Win-Win Solution

What makes any kind of added-value selling work is that it is a win-win situation. This is probably one of the greatest clichés of selling, and one of the truest. Both parties should come to a sales situation feeling that they've gained something. If you have clearly positioned your product or service, you will reap the financial rewards of the transaction. But the other side will have solved a problem or met a challenge. So both parties are accomplishing their objectives.

With all the pressure on you as a sales rep to perform and to make your quotas, it's not always easy to focus on building relationships and win-win situations. Therefore, your most challenging task is to make sure you don't lose sight of the real objective. Once you reduce the game to just numbers, and it becomes nothing more than making your quota and earning your commission, you lose the joy and fun of selling. The people who are most successful get the most satisfaction out of creating win-win situations. They take pride in a job well done and in helping somebody else, knowing that they will be rewarded for it in the end. Instead of looking at their job and saying, "How am I going to hit this number? I'd better call ABC Company and push something on them," high achievers look at it from another angle. They say, "I know ABC Company has this challenge in front of them, and I know I can help them solve it."

That philosophy also helps you determine when a win-win situation is not possible. Not every situation is ideal. There are times when you may present a viable solution to a customer who, for one reason or another, is not willing or able to see its value. Those are the times you have to walk away from the business.

If a particular customer can't get beyond the price issue, it may be a signal to move on. Sales reps waste a lot of time on prospects that are not qualified, don't have the decision-making ability, or are stalling them along. Most often, the reason reps discount the price is because they're desperate for a sale. They need the account so badly that they're willing to do almost anything to get it. Because of their lack of activity and new prospects, they'll sacrifice the value of the product by discounting just to get a deal. When that happens, everyone suffers. It's a lose-lose situation, and it usually ends up with everyone, including the customer, being dissatisfied with the outcome.

"There are some customers who want to test you to see what you will do," says Dan Berger of Coca-Cola Enterprises. "They tell

> *"To give real service you must add something which cannot be bought or measured with money, and that is sincerity and integrity."*
>
> —Douglas Adams

you that they're getting a great deal from one of your competitors. At that point, you may just have to say, 'If you can get that deal, you should probably take it.' Half the time the customer is bluffing, and will call you back later to accept your proposal. In the long run, the more they see that you're really trying to help their business, the more they'll trust you and eventually buy from you.

"But it can't be a win-lose situation for you. I've even seen salespeople create lose-win situations, where they wanted the deal so badly they were actually losing money. They were selling to the customer at less than cost! Then, when they tried to get a price increase, the customer complained, because all they were sold was price. There wasn't any value or loyalty built there."

[Six Steps *to* Building Value]

Most salespeople understand the theory behind selling value: that you're not only selling a particular product or service, but are also selling a complete package that includes quality products, customer service, and your own honesty, integrity, and unique ability to help solve customers' problems. But when a customer brings up a price objection, salespeople are tempted to take the easiest route to the close, which is to sell at a discount or even below cost.

Here are six steps to help you sell value without dropping price.

1. Go back to basics.

Georgette Ravell is vice president of sales and marketing at O'Connor-Ravell Associates, a New Jersey–based commercial collection agency. What does her company have to offer clients that other companies don't? For her, value starts with the basics.

"One of the most valuable assets we have is our reputation for being ethical," she says. "The collection business can be a 'dirty' one. But fifty percent of all our new accounts come from referrals—because our current customers know they can rely on us for honesty and candor, as well as results."

The company recently formed a collection division alliance partnership with NACM/Chicago-Midwest that made O'Connor-Ravell one of the largest revenue-producing agencies in the United States. "Other companies were pursuing this alliance," says Ravell, "but we didn't even know about it. They called us—based on our outstanding reputation—and when the deal went through, we literally doubled the size of our company in two weeks."

It takes effort to build that kind of reputation. "It's the small things that add up to a great reputation," adds Ravell. "For instance, we believe in personal communication. There is no voice mail in our company (except when the offices are closed). Your questions and concerns are answered immediately, by a real live person."

2. Listen, listen, listen.

Use all of the listening skills you have to probe for more information than a customer may be willing to give initially. It's especially important to listen for the customer's hot buttons—those things that are really important to him. You want to determine how your product or service can address those hot buttons. By answering these concerns, you will be able to add value for this customer.

3. Offer continual reinforcement.

Customers need to know that you are on the same track as they are. They don't want any surprises. Use pinpointing questions, such as "What you're saying, Mr. Customer, is that you need immediate delivery. Is that right?" or "I want to be sure I understand you. You have ten computer stations that need to be networked. Is that correct?" This reinforcement reassures customers that you listened to and understood their problems, which automatically increases your value.

4. Get your customers to sell value for you.

Nothing sells better than a satisfied customer—especially one who went to the competition for a lower price but came back to you because he didn't get the service he expected. Make a tape recording of a customer telling his story, or have him write it out on his letterhead. I've made many sales because I made the initial effort of interviewing some of my key customers, asking them why they bought from me, what other companies they considered, and what added value they got after doing business with me. That way, when other customers question your price, you can say, "I appreciate that, but I'd like you to hear from somebody who felt that there were competitors out there who were less expensive. But they ended up buying from us and here's why. . . ." Then you can play them the tape or hand them the testimonial letter so they can see (or hear) for themselves that the added value really exists. This is another way of differentiating yourself from other salespeople.

5. Find out what is most important besides price.

What are the key criteria, or hot buttons, for this customer, besides price? He might say, "We need widgets that can be delivered to us within two days of an order," or "We need a widget that can withstand the rough environment of our factory floor." The better your product or service matches these factors, the less likely it is that price will be the deciding factor. Price is important, but make sure you're well versed in the other areas you might deliver on better than the competition.

6. Deliver more than you promise.

There's nothing unusual about a company stating that customer service is its number-one priority. Most companies these days make that statement. So if you want to stand out with your customers, you've got to go beyond that promise and deliver more than just standard service.

Take, for example, this story from Pat Bruggeman, senior manager for consumer sales training at Gateway Computers: "My assistant, Angie Bunker, previously worked in customer service. Two years ago, she answered the phone to find a frantic customer on the other end. It was Christmastime, and it seemed that Gateway had accidentally double-billed the customer for a computer. The reason the customer was so upset was that because of that error, she had reached the spending limit on her credit card. She had no more funds with which to buy her children gifts for the holiday.

"Angie spent a long time on the phone with the customer, assuring her that the mistake would be rectified. She also calmed her down by asking about her children and what they wanted for Christmas. That evening, Angie and her husband went out shopping and used their own money to buy gifts for this customer's kids. They sent them overnight so that she would have them in time for Christmas.

"Needless to say, we now have a customer for life. The customer called Angie's supervisor to sing her praises, and wrote a letter to the CEO. The customer has relayed this story to all her friends and family, and has brought in many more customers to Gateway. I'm not sure you can find a better example of delivering more than you promise."

Those are just some of the ways to build value beyond price. It's also important to understand the difference between price and cost. Price is what customers pay to purchase your product or service. Cost is what they're going to pay over the lifetime of your relationship. So while your initial price may be higher than the competition's, the lifetime cost will be lower because of the high standards of quality and service you offer as added value.

The Value *of* Learning *from* Your Mistakes

No matter how hard you try to provide perfect service for customers, mistakes are bound to happen. The fact that you have made a mistake won't necessarily count against you. It's what you do after the mistake that matters. What many people don't realize is that mistakes are opportunities to prove yourself and to become even more valuable to your customers. You can examine what you did wrong and avoid making those mistakes again. It's been said that if someone has had a good experience with a store or a salesperson, they'll tell nine people. If they had a bad experience, they'll tell twelve people. So if you do the math, you can see you're going to be in trouble if you don't continue to provide the best customer service. Customers don't expect you to be perfect, but they do expect you to be responsive.

This is a lesson that Val-Pak's Ann Hanford personally learned. She believes that if you make a mistake, first you have to admit it, and then do whatever you can to rectify the situation. Once, Hanford put together an ad for a client's cellular phone business. The ad was supposed to read, "200 minutes for $39.95; 1,000 minutes for $99.95." Instead, thousands of ads were sent out reading, "20,000 minutes for $39.95; 100,000 minutes for $99.95."

Naturally, the client was angry, but Hanford went down to his business and helped him answer the phone to let people know of the printing error. He was so impressed that she had come to help him that all he asked for was a $50 credit. "It's a mistake that I won't make again," says Hanford, "but my customer appreciated that I was there to help him through the situation."

> *"The greatest mistake a man can make is to be afraid of making one."*
>
> —ELBERT HUBBARD

[Ask *for* Feedback]

Most of the time, your customers don't tell you how you're doing. There's only one way to find out: ask them. Look for problems. Look for your areas of weakness so that you can improve them. There are several ways you can get this feedback:

- ❑ **Conduct phone or mail surveys.** Given the opportunity, most customers are more than willing to give you feedback about how you and your company are doing. You can either call your customers or send them (short) printed surveys to fill out and mail back. Ask questions like:

- Why did you decide to go with our company?
- Whom else did you look at before going with our company?
- What can I or my company do to generate more business from you?
- How can we improve the products or service you currently use, to help you improve your business?
- What are the three most important things we can do as a vendor to keep our relationship strong?
- What do you like best about our company?
- What do you like least about our company?
- Is there anything I should be doing that I'm not doing now?

❑ **Bring customers in to see your operation.** Some companies bring customers in to tour their facilities so that they can understand and appreciate their business. The Marriott hotel chain, for example, invites meeting planners to stay at one of their facilities and meet everyone on their staff so that the planners can learn their business from the inside—and so that people who don't normally meet the customers (chefs, reservationists, catering) can hear feedback directly from customers.

❏ **Think like a customer.** Treat your customer's business as if it were your own. Learn the industry's issues and jargon. Be your customer's advocate at your company meetings. Thinking like a customer can help you anticipate problems before they occur and differentiate you from your competitors.

❏ **Listen in on customer service calls.** If you listen to real customers calling your company, it enables you to find out firsthand the type of problems they actually run into, and to understand how these problems do (or do not) get solved.

Customers are sometimes reluctant to give feedback on their own, because they feel there's not much they can do about unsatisfactory service. You can change that perception, not only by giving your customers the best quality and service, but also by giving them a voice in setting the high standards they desire—and deserve.

Whether your customer is one individual or a corporate conglomerate, your number-one priority is creating value. You must create a relationship so strong—based on your essential value to that customer's business—that they won't leave you to go to a competitor. You have to move beyond the role of a supplier of a product or service, and become your customer's business partner.

CHAPTER RECAP:

YOU GET WHAT YOU PAY FOR

[
This cliché means that when a customer buys something from a successful salesperson, no matter what they pay for it, they'll get their money's worth—in fact, they'll get more.
]

Ways to add value.

- Differentiate yourself.
- Offer excellence and creativity, and get involved with the community.
- An added-value approach helps you become one of your customer's assets.

The value of the win-win solution.

- What makes added-value selling work is that it is a win-win situation.
- The most successful salespeople take pride in a job well done and in helping other people, knowing they will be rewarded in the end.
- Be careful not to create lose-win situations just to get the sale.

Six steps to building value:

1. Go back to basics.
2. Listen, listen, listen.
3. Continually reinforce customers' buying decisions.
4. Get your customers to sell value for you.
5. Find out what is most important besides price.
6. Deliver more than you promise.

The value of learning from your mistakes.

- The fact that you make a mistake won't necessarily count against you; it's what you do after the mistake that counts.
- Mistakes are opportunities to prove yourself and to become even more valuable to your customers.
- Customers don't expect you to be perfect, but they do expect you to be responsive.

Ask your customers for feedback.

- Look for your areas of weakness so that you can improve them.
- Get this feedback by:
  - Conducting phone or mail surveys.
  - Bringing customers in to see your operation.
  - Thinking like a customer.
  - Listening in on customer service calls.

12 Honesty Is *the* Best Policy

Imagine that you've just made a sale. A big sale to Crusty Custom Candies, the prospect you've been pursuing for eight months. You've got lots of plans for the money this will bring in. You have an appointment for 10:00 A.M. tomorrow to sign the papers and close the deal. As you go over the details in your mind for the hundredth time, you're suddenly shocked to realize that you've made a mistake. The price you quoted Mr. Crusty was for Model B, not Model A, which is the one he wanted.

What do you do? You could go ahead and close the deal and ship him Model B. There's not that much difference between the two models anyway; he probably won't even notice the

> *"No legacy is so rich as honesty."*
>
> —WILLIAM SHAKESPEARE,
> ALL'S WELL THAT ENDS WELL

difference. If he does, you can always say it was a typo in the contract; you can blame it on your secretary. You can close the deal and ship him Model A and take a loss on the deal. Or you can call him up, explain your error, and find out if he wants to reopen negotiations.

Which option would you choose?

Do you really have to think about it?

This one should be a no-brainer. In fact, in an ideal world, there would be no need for this chapter at all. Options one and two wouldn't even exist. This is not, however, an ideal world, and certainly not an ideal sales world. The vast majority of salespeople are hardworking and ethical. But honest salespeople have long had to suffer the stigma of the con men and hucksters who have been known to populate this profession. Who can blame a customer for being overly cautious or for not wanting to make hasty buying decisions?

[Beware *the* Slippery Slope]

Most customers are savvier today, but suckers are still born every minute. There will always be someone to fool. Some people actually believe they've won a sweepstakes when they get a letter that says, "John Doe, you have won $10 million!," and then in small print, "if your lucky number matches the winning sequence. . . ." Some people invest in stock schemes thinking they can get rich quick and live out their lives on easy street. And behind those schemes and scams there are unscrupulous salespeople who are somehow able to look themselves in the mirror every morning.

"But those salespeople are the exceptions to the rule," you might be saying. "They are few and far between." Maybe so. But what about the many instances every day when a salesperson "forgets" to add in the delivery charge, or doesn't disclose some other fine-print add-on? In reality, there are many small and subtle opportunities for salespeople to be dishonest every day.

Joe Kubala, district manager for Trane Company, a manufacturer of commercial and industrial air-conditioning products, once found himself with such an opportunity. It was at the beginning of his career, and he was a salesperson in Connecticut. He had just begun to develop a relationship with a customer who said that he would buy ten coils (parts for his product) at a total cost of $3,800. When the purchase order arrived, however, it was for $38,000. It would have been possible to put the order through. But Kubala quickly called the customer and related the error.

"That became the basis for a long and financially rewarding relationship," says Kubala. "These people knew they could trust me to do the right thing, and they showed their appreciation by becoming one of our best customers."

There are many areas of life that are more shades of gray than black and white, but honesty is not one of them. You just do the right thing. Sometimes, we consider not doing the right thing because we don't want people to discover that we're not perfect—that we're somehow less worthy of others' respect. But everyone makes mistakes, and most often people respect you more when you have the courage to admit your error.

Customers appreciate a sales rep who is straightforward, who lays his cards out on the table. Nobody wants to be faced with unpleasant surprises, and nobody wants to feel that they've been scammed. Customers can forgive mistakes; they will not forgive lies. If a product doesn't have the features they need, they want to be told that up front. If a service is going to cost more than they want to pay, there is only one way to deal with the situation—lay the fact out on the line.

That's just what Kelly Harman, vice president of Wire One Technologies, did when she got a phone call from a man looking to buy videoconferencing equipment. The caller had obtained information from another vendor and wanted to get a competitive bid. Before they began to talk price, Harman asked him questions about his company and how they were planning to use the equipment he was thinking of buying. She soon realized that he thought the equipment would do more than it could actually do.

"I had to tell him that the system he was considering could not meet his company's needs," says Harman. "Not only that, I told him we could not meet the other vendor's price on that equipment. I explained exactly what the system could do and just how much it would cost."

After several phone conversations, Harman sent this prospect an alternate system she felt would better suit his needs, with no obligation to buy, so that he could test it out and see for himself what it could or could not do.

"He ended up buying three systems from me, even though they cost more than he would have paid for them from my competitor," says Harman, "only because in our first conversation, I was not afraid to tell him that he wasn't going to be able to get what he wanted. He's now a good customer, and we have a terrific working relationship."

Your goal is always to build relationships; how can you do that if you're not honest? Selling is really a matter of building trust, and once that happens, the actual sale is almost a by-product.

The Philosophy Behind *the* Cliché

People often make excuses for bad behavior by saying, "It's only business." There is no such thing. The values you live by at home are the same ones you use to conduct business. Here are three values that help maintain integrity in life.

1. Seek truth in everything you do.
Believe that what you do has value. Understand the benefits that

you bring to people with your product or service, and with the way that you conduct yourself. Know that every decision you make involves a choice: you can maintain your honesty and your core values, or you can chip away at your own beliefs by giving in to temptations (large and small). There have been projects I have been offered over the years that might have made me large sums of money, but they were not projects I believed in. I turned them down and was poorer, perhaps, but happier that I did.

Every day, it is your job to stand in front of your prospect or customer with total commitment and belief in what you do. Your belief in your product or service and your belief in yourself help you sell with passion. That passion gives you great persuasive power as a salesperson. If your product is not a panacea, don't claim that it is.

You are asking your customer to make an investment that directly or indirectly involves his money, his shareholders, his employees, and his livelihood, and he's doing this because he believes in you. It is therefore necessary for you to be equally strong in your belief that what you are doing is worthy of that customer's investment.

2. Seek truth in others.

First, look for the good in others. There is something good in everyone, if you take the time to get to know the person and understand what is important to him or her. You can't do that if you view everyone as nothing more than a potential source of income. You can't form a meaningful relationship with a bank account or a paycheck; you can form meaningful relationships only with individuals who have unique needs and goals. And it's those individual relationships that lead to sales.

There will be some people, however, whose goodness is difficult to find, and it is your job to stay away from them—whether they are customers or employers. Some customers want you to cut special deals for them. They want you to be dishonest to your other customers or to your company. They are interested only in their own benefit, and try to convince you their schemes will profit you as well. If you have enough activity going on, you won't even have to stop to consider this kind of business. You will simply say, "No thanks," and move on to other prospects.

> *"The naked truth is always better than the best-dressed lie."*
>
> —*Ann Landers*

Then there are some companies that don't value a salesperson's integrity. They want you to get the sale no matter what it takes. They think that fraud and deception are effective sales tools. If you find yourself in this atmosphere, no matter where you find it, get out. The money may be tempting; these kinds of operations usually play for high stakes. But it's not worth the price of your soul. As Zig Ziglar once said, "It's impossible to make a good deal with bad people."

3. Value your integrity.
Stand on your principles and they will keep you upright. Speak

well of others that they might speak well of you. If a customer starts to bad-mouth your competition, don't agree with her. Just say, "I don't know what you might have heard about them, but here's what makes our company unique. . . ." If you don't know the company your customer is disparaging, just say, again, "I'm not familiar with that company, but here's what makes us different from others in our industry. . . ." Focus on what's positive about you and your product, rather than what's negative about someone else's. When you're throwing dirt at somebody else, all you're doing is digging out your own foundation. It is not necessary to tear someone else down in order to build yourself up. It is necessary only to remain true to yourself and your purpose in life.

[The Truth Is *in the* Doing]

Each one of us is born with amazing gifts. Your purpose in life is to discover what those gifts are and to explore them every single day. One way to do that is to keep expanding the things you do.

Being a salesperson is a great job. You get to meet a lot of interesting, intelligent people in a variety of settings. You get to be creative and to express your personality. You get to experiment constantly with the way you do things, and find methods of improving your productivity.

There are many things in life that complement selling. I find that almost everything I do leads me to a greater understanding of myself and the people around me, which, when applied, leads to greater sales success. Tae Kwon Do, for example, has taught me many new ways of viewing situations. It has set me off in new directions I didn't even know existed, so that I have seen personal growth that has enabled me to bring new value to my customers.

In the end, life is a flow. If you want to change the flow of your life, you can, by making honest choices that move you toward a specific goal. As I discovered while writing my fifth book, *Diamond in the Rough,* the most successful people do not end their lives by counting their money and their material possessions. They look back at their lives and ask, "How much did I love? How much did I learn?" These are the important questions.

If you're honest with yourself, you will end each day by asking, "Did I give one hundred percent effort in everything I did today? Did I really listen to my customers? Did I find out what their needs and concerns were, and did I discover what I could do to match those needs? Do I have enough activity going on to be seeding for the future, or am I coasting along on a few successful accounts?"

If you want to find the truth, you find it in the doing. You truly know something only through your experience of it. Honest success comes from going out there and calling on customers, and from picking up the phone and making the calls.

That is the only way to find the methods that will work best for you with many different types of customers. You can't sell from someone else's experience. Your truth has to be based on who you are and how you experience the world.

Honesty comes from getting past your fears, from doing those things that help you learn about yourself and your place in the world. It leads to the path with heart, the one that speaks to you with certainty that this is the right way. There is no excuse for thinking, "I've just got to do whatever it takes to make this one deal, and I'll be honest on the next one." Every deal must be based on your understanding of how to benefit others. If it is not, you are not only cheating your customers, but also cheating yourself.

Honesty *is* the best policy. This is a basic truth of life, and it remains true no matter how many times we hear it. The problem with clichés is that we've heard them so often, we don't pay attention to them anymore. But we should. We should remind ourselves of them every day and implement them in fresh, new ways.

The next time you hear a cliché, don't be so quick to dismiss it. Look for the truth in it. We all know the things that make us better salespeople, and better people. Sometimes, though, we just need to be reminded.

CHAPTER RECAP:
HONESTY IS *the* BEST POLICY

[
*Customers are smarter and savvier
than ever before. They expect to be
sold on a personal, realistic basis.*
]

Beware the slippery slope.

- It's easy to excuse oneself for little dishonesties, but it is a slippery slope; little deceptions can turn into big lies.
- People respect you more when you have the courage to admit your errors.
- Selling is a matter of building trust.

The philosophy behind the cliché.

- Seek truth in everything you do.
- Seek truth in others.
- Value your integrity.

The truth is in the doing.

- Your purpose in life is to discover your particular gifts and explore them every day.
- Be honest with yourself—end each day by asking, "Did I give one hundred percent effort in everything I did today?"
- Honesty comes from taking a path with heart.